mainely lake life

RAMP-AGE TO RAMBUNCTIOUS

RON DESCOTEAUX

KNOTTY LOON

contents

BAUNEG BEG LAKE
SANFORD — N. BERWICK
MAINE

Map updated September 2022 by Ron and Jeannine Descoteaux,
Anne Whitten, and Maine Busson-Forfait
Lorraine Brown, President

Bauneg Beg Lake

SANFORD

NORTH BERWICK

Route 4 (Country Club Rd.)

Sandy Beach
Loon Cove (2016)
Maria Cove (1908)
CAUTION
Breezy Point
Otter Cove
Echo Beach
Huckleberry Point (1908)
Crows Nest
Clark Cove
Pine Needle Point
Green Head Bay (2022)
Birch Cove
Grover's Cove (1908)
Grover's Point
Blueberry Island (1908)
Kiss Island
R Windy Way Point (2022)
Poole's Point
Corbin Way
Patriots Cove (2016)
Turtle/Brody's Island
Turtle Cove
Sunset Strip
Hammock Island
Cobb Cove
Mosquito Cove (1908)
Cobb Cove Way
The River

Cutaway Dr.
Oak Hill Rd.
Sunny Ln.
Emile Ln.
Shout Ln.
Fern Ln.
Jessica Ln.
Chestnut Sanford Service
Kennebec Ln.
Balsam Ln.
Chestnut Ln.
Abenaki Ln.

N
W   E
S

0   500   1,020

welcome readers

Whether this is your first introduction to my books, or if you've been a faithful follower, welcome to the fifth edition of short lakeside memoirs. I've been writing these true to life stories for more than 20 years, never thinking that one day I would be sharing them with you, yet.... here we are. Every story is true with maybe a slight bit of embellishment. What started out as a hobby to share with my family and friends only has become a real gift I can share with you. I only ask one thing. That you have a sense of humor! Yeah, that's important.

It was back in the early spring of 1995 that my wife and I purchased our lake house in southern Maine. It was a dream come true for us. While most folks save their money for 50 weeks a year so they can go on a two-week vacation somewhere, in buying the cottage, we found ourselves on a semi-permanent vacation all year long. And what a trip this has been.

When we purchased our little piece of heaven, little did we know we were also getting a ringside seat to the best area of the lake. Being one house removed, we have the best view of the busy (and only) boat ramp. While our lake has no public access, local marinas and many lake residents use the private ramp to launch their prized possessions. During the busy season I find myself enjoying the goings-on from my perch on the main deck, usually reading a novel from my favorite author, and with a cold refreshing beverage not far away, all the while lounging in my zero-gravity recliner. (Why do they call it that? I have the worse time getting out of those. But, I digress.) And from my perch, the often humorous and unforgettable stories take shape for you and me to enjoy.

The stories in this book are based on actual events that I have personally witnessed or been part of. These same stories depict events and circumstances that happen at any lake in this beautiful country. If you're fortunate enough to live on a lake or pond, then you'll see what may happen in your neck of the woods. Some of the stories may not describe wholly the events as they took place, but whatever I omitted or embellished wasn't important enough to change the story itself. The stories refer to some characters who live here on the lake, and others who are just visiting. You will meet them as you read through the stories. For some, I use their lake persona and do so with the greatest respect for their friendship and willingness to be part of these adventures. Others are just that, characters.

I found that if I can (and do) laugh at myself every day, then I can allow myself some poetic license to interpret my friends and neighbors in how I perceive them, given the circumstances they find themselves in. I wouldn't trade my lake neighbors for anyone.

I hope you will find some humor and enjoyment in these stories. I wrote them for the love of writing, though I don't consider myself a writer. Being able to share these stories with you is a gift in itself, a legacy for my family. I hope you enjoy the adventure. So... let's get started.

from where it comes

T 've always said that living near the Corbin Way boat ramp was the place of entertainment for me. Year after year, story after story, I've never been disappointed. From my sturdy perch overlooking the warm waters of this beautiful lake, I have a firsthand account of the constant shenanigans, misadventures, faux pas, and other discombobulated tomfoolery that goes on (and on) at or near the ramp. I know that last sentence doesn't blend well with our modern language, but when you drink vodka and Coke... yeah, it does! When I think I've seen it all, friends and visitors on the lake using the ramp always leave me with warm memories. Or is that warmth from the vodka? Either way, here we go!

Recently, a truck backed a boat trailer into the shallow waters of the boat ramp. I was relaxing on the deck under the warm azure blue sky, sipping a cold beverage, when a disturbance took me out of the Indian Ocean where I was helping Dirk Pitt locate a sunken treasure. Soon, a small power boat came around Windy Way Point and headed for the trailer that was already in the water waiting to retrieve its load. The boat operator approached the sunken trailer and boarded the trailer bunks easily. I thought, *This guy is really good*. Then, for whatever reason, he decided to disembark the trailered boat while it was

1

still in the water. He climbed on the port (left side) gunnel (top edge of the boat), sat and dropped off the boat. The guy was about 5-foot 6-inches tall, and he dropped into a 4-foot deep section of the ramp. He landed nearly chest high in the cool water with his sweatshirt now up around his neck. I wondered what he was thinking, getting out of the dry boat. The driver would have easily pulled the trailer and its load safely to dry land. I guess he wanted one last swim for the year. It didn't look like he enjoyed it at all. Me.... I sure was enjoying my beverage. Luckily, I had a bookmark on page 256 of my novel. Dirk Pitt needed my help. At least Dirk wore a wet suit!

The next day, another pontoon boat was getting ready to call it a season and leave the lake bed. A pickup truck had backed a long trailer down the road into the shallow waters of the ramp, waiting to retrieve its load. The boat and operator slowly approached the sunken trailer, which proved to be smart, since his first try missed the carpeted bunks altogether, causing him to back out and try again. On the second attempt, he promptly missed the trailer as a minor breeze pushed the canopied boat off course. Backing out, he needed a third try. Again, he missed the mark, and again backed out for another run at the trailer. I had time to refresh my beverage as this painful event was not going to end soon. I wondered if he had enough fuel for this escapade. Try as he might, the boat was again either pulled to one side, or slid off the bunks and, on another attempt, hit the front upright post of the trailer holding the winch. After the sixth or seventh try, he finally made it on the trailer long enough for the driver to haul him to dry land. That was painful to watch, but just enough time for me to enjoy another beverage. Maybe I should have invited him over for a drink.... I think he needed one!

A more unusual event caught my attention recently. A friend of mine drove his pontoon boat to the ramp one late morning, tying it off to a nearby tree on shore. I walked over to see him and he told me he was pulling his boat out. Knowing he lived 875.9655 yards up the road, I offered to give him a ride home to get his trailer. (Actually it was 875.9685 yards) So, off we went. I dropped him off, knowing I would see him again soon. Within a few minutes, he showed up with his pontoon trailer, being pulled by a shiny John Deere tractor. *Well*, I thought, *this is different*. I asked if he needed help, but said he was "fine" and could get the boat easily trailered. So, I stood back to watch him work. Some folks enjoy the challenge, and here I was without a beverage. Once the trailer was in the water where he wanted it, he returned to the boat and walked it over behind the trailer and slowly pulled the 16-foot platform party boat unto the trailer bunks, where he methodically hooked up the winch strap to the nose of the boat and expertly cranked the boat up on the trailer to its stops. He easily drove the tractor and its load to dry land. Then he waved me good bye and headed home with his pontoon boat in tow behind the shiny John Deere tractor. Me... I returned to the cottage for a refreshing beverage. That long ride to his house and back sure did work up a serious thirst.

Speaking of a first, this one was most unusual. Well, so far anyway. While I was out enjoying a beef burrito at a local Mexican watering hole, another friend texted me and asked me if he could use my beach as a "pit stop" until he could get there to remove it from the lake. I was thinking of his pontoon boat, of course. When I got home, I didn't see anything nearby. So I reached out and asked him if he changed his mind. He said, "No, it's floating near the ramp and I'm waiting for the wife to get home and I'll come get it with my trailer." I looked over toward the right of way, but saw nothing that caught my eye. And I still had good vision, despite the Margarita El Grande I had to wash down that burrito. Being curious, I walked over to the ramp and saw what he was talking about. There, floating in the water, tied off to a small bush, was a pile of eight stacked up wooden dock tops, nicely bundled together for removal. Really? A pile of wood? The pile was 4 feet by 8 feet and was the tops to his wooden docking system. He used the tops as a walkway near his cottage during the winter to provide a safer walking area. Clever!

A few minutes after I got there, I heard his car backing down with the trailer he used for his sailboat. After a pleasant greeting, he backed the trailer into the shallow ramp and promptly jackknifed it sharply to his right. Then again on the second try, until he found it easier to just pick up the rear end of the trailer and walk it to the center of the ramp. I offered to go in the water and help, but he assured me that he had this. He untied the wooden stack and walked it to the rear of the trailer like he would his pontoon boat. In minutes, he had attached the trailer's winch to a knotted front sling, and with little effort, he hand-cranked the two-foot high load of heavy, wet docking onto the trailer. He checked the loads placement on the trailer before driving up Corbin Way and headed home. Nice job neighbor! Sometimes, people just wow me!

loon or loony

I am a reactionary. I am not a procrastinator! When things tend to need attention, and I can make a difference, then I'm on the case like a fat person on a bucket of KFC! Extra crispy! Such was the case in the middle of June when a public clatter arose from the lake residents concerning our feathered friends, the common loon. Although, along the shores of this beautiful lake, they are anything but common. Each year, the mating pair of black and white feathered birds grace the 200-acre lake much to the delight of its many residents.

Almost each day, they are photographed with their photos appearing on social media so that a constant "eyes on" is witnessed to their wellbeing. Once the baby loons, usually two, are born, their popularity brings further attention.

However, in the middle of June, several incidents of nefarious intent were witnessed near the loon sanctuary on Lollipop Island. One incident involved some careless pet owner who let his dog out on the island to relieve himself while the stressed out nesting birds stood off watching, hoping their babies would remain safe. They were! I think we should relieve ourselves of the thoughtless person who allowed his animal to defecate on the island. Did he pick it up? I think not!

On another occasion, another intruder felt it necessary to go on the island to take pictures of the loon nest and the eggs. What are people thinking? These two incidents, happening within a short time frame, prompted the social media to light up with concerned outrage. One person indicated that the buoy master (me, unfortunately) should take appropriate action to protect the loon nest before tragedy befalls the loon family, and further upset the lake residents, and thus avoiding a gang uprising against known offenders. So, I went to work, promising to take action at the site before the Fourth of July weekend when too many outsiders grace our shores and care less for our feathered friends. I had four days to act... and I went to work.

Not having any buoy making material available here, I proceeded to go to the men's toy store, or Lowe's for everyone else. Having premeasured the state buoys, I knew I was looking for five-inch diameter plastic piping, or PVC for connoisseurs of fine plumbing. Getting to the right aisle and bin, I found the correct piping. A five-foot length was tagged at $33. WHAT!?! I needed three lengths and that meant six 5-inch caps to seal the ends. Those were even more expensive, pricing out at $15 each. High prices, all in the name of Covid-19, supply issues, and the all-American greed! But what choice did I have? The loons needed protecting. So, I bought the nearly $200 in plastic supplies, along with 3-inch black vinyl lettering along with some minor hardware and went home to assemble the three buoys that would keep the loon sanctuary safe from... well... whoever.

Once at home, the lovely First Mate went to work lettering the piping with vertical letters announcing, "LOONS NESTING" and beneath that, horizontally, "KEEP AWAY". After completing the three buoys, we were proud of our work and couldn't wait to launch them at the site, thus keeping the birds safe. Next, I took the three buoys out to the workshop and installed the steel eye bolts to the bottom of one cap, to which I would attach the chain to the anchor. Once made, I was ready to seal one end of the 5-inch tube. Looking around, I had no PVC cement to do any sealing with. Crap! So, off to Lowe's once again for a small can of PVC cement. On my return, I finally got one cap sealed.

The State buoys are weighted on the low end to help the buoys float upright when properly anchored in the water. Having an extra state buoy in my possession, I weighed it on my bathroom scale. It came in at twenty-three pounds. So I filled the open end of my new buoy with rock and sand until it weighed the right amount, then sealed the top with another cap. Buoy #1 done and ready for action. I thought to myself, *Maybe I should go out front near my dock and see how well the buoy floats before I go any further.* It looked very professional and weighed the right amount, and I had little doubt in my buoy-making, loon-protecting, public-pleasing skills.

I waded out into about four feet of water and stood the buoy up and let it go. It fell over sideways faster than an Irishman leaving a bar on St. Patrick's Day. (Hey, it could happen!) I was a little disappointed. So I removed the top cap and proceeded (unsuccessfully) to add and remove weight until I found a happy medium where the buoy would float. Try as I might, after six attempts, I was flummoxed! Bamboozled! Discombobulated! Flabbergasted! You get the point, right? All this money, and I couldn't float a 5-inch sealed pipe! Back to the drawing board.

Seeing my buoy was not being buoyant, my neighbor came to assist in the project. After several more tries, we decided that I had the 5-inch tube right, but the length might be making a difference. The state buoys were 77 inches in length and mine were only 60 inches. If a 60-inch buoy was $33, how much more would a 77-inch buoy cost? Since the State buoys were engineered... that was probably the answer to my vexing problem. I had had enough for one day, and decided the next day would bring success. So, I had a vodka and Coke and forgot (nearly) the miseries of my long summer day! Thank you, neighbor!

The next morning, with my healthy attitude in full swing, I returned to the toy store for more pipe and more fittings. This time I figured that one section of pipe would be all I needed to make each of the three buoys 77 inches long. Another $33! Then I needed couplings so I could make the splice work out to the right numbers. I should have brought my vodka with me when I stared at the staggering price of $18 per coupling. I offered to work the cash register for four hours to pay for the couplings, but was told they only use self checkout now! Screwed again!

With my expensive parts in hand, I returned to the workshop and started modifying the first buoy. I cut the weighted bottom section and fitted it with one of the couplings. Then I measured the 17 inches I needed, keeping the coupling length in mind. After a dry fit, the buoy measured 77.184648 inches. Close enough! Sorry, that was 77.184645 inches. No wonder I make mistakes. Once I was satisfied that I had the correct height and weight, I took my trusty can of PVC cement (glue) and put the buoy together, letting it dry hard for about 15 minutes. I felt good about it this time. (I really should have had more vodka!).

Once again, I took the reengineered buoy out to the dock and waded in to about four feet of water and let the buoy go. For a minute I thought I needed to drink more, but then, the 5-inch buoy started bobbing like an apple at a Halloween Party. I was giddy with joy. I think I actually peed in the water. Okay, that was improper, but at seventy-three, I can usually pee anytime, and I was already wet, and there was no one around. I was happy! About the buoy, I mean!

It was now midafternoon, and I had plenty of time to go launch the new buoy and see how it would do onsite. So, I boarded the 20-foot pontoon with my first newly engineered buoy, 6 feet of chain and my concrete anchor. Getting near Lollipop Island (Loon Sanctuary), I picked a site some 40 feet from the island and set the buoy off the front of the boat, where it lollygagged for a second, then came upright and floated like it was supposed to. I was overjoyed at the sight. I was ready to head back and reengineer the other two buoys and get the project done. The hard work was paying off!

Returning to the workshop, I commenced to cut, fit, and glue the remaining materials into two more 77-inch buoys that would grace Lollipop Island, make a nautical fashion statement, and put the project to rest, and more importantly, keep our little birds safe from traffic of any kind. I happily worked on finishing up the last two buoys, anxious to get out there and complete the project. I was thinking that maybe I could sell the loon buoy idea to the state and put our little lake on the map with this nautical innovation.

I loaded my two new reengineered lake buoys on the boat with anchors and chain and my first mate and I set out for Lollipop Island, feeling relaxed and content that the work was finally coming to an end. We took a slow cruise to the site, enjoying the day as we traveled south. I was as happy as Gilligan finding a way off the island. On approaching the loon sanctuary, I said to The First Mate, "Where the heck is my buoy?" It was nowhere to be seen. Had someone removed it? I looked around to make sure it hadn't floated off, although that wasn't likely. Surveying the area, The First Mate suddenly called out, "Two points off the starboard bow, that's where she sits in Davey Jones' locker!" My buoy had sunk, still floating erect... but sunk in a shallow grave, the top cap one foot below the surface.

I knew I had to retrieve the sunken buoy as it would surely cause a danger to navigation. The First Mate took the helm and began an approach on the buoy, while I laid prone on the deck trying to reach underwater to grab the top of the buoy and hoist it aboard the boat. We tried several times, but the wind kept us at bay. Frustrations were growing, and here I was without a single drop of grog... I mean vodka. A new plan was quickly developed.

The First Mate got a life jacket from the storage locker and ordered me over the side. I jumped in with a section of ½ inch braided nylon line in my hand, intending to lasso the top of the buoy and let The First Mate haul it in. The water was a warm seventy-four degrees, and I was very comfortable in the water. After several tries, I finally manage to wrangle the buoy onboard, wondering why it sank to begin with. It looked promising when I launched it two hours earlier.

As we hauled the buoy in, I noticed it was much heavier than when I launched it. We soon found the buoy had filled with water from the leaks on the couplings and the lower cap. There was no sense launching the other two, knowing they would meet the same watery demise. Back to the dock and the workshop.

Since I had little time left and was a little discouraged from the past two days' efforts, I improvised. I had three state hazard buoys in storage for spares, so I rigged those three buoys with chain and anchors, returned to Lollipop Island, and deployed those three buoys around the nesting site. They floated perfectly as I expected and would serve as warnings for boaters and others to remain clear of the small island in the middle of the lake.

Being the current Buoy Master, and as required by the State Navigation Office, I reported the issue, and the buoy launch to the state. I was told that the three buoys I had in place were not legally enforceable because of the location. However, since they were for temporary use and would be removed within two weeks, I could use them.

NOTE: The State of Maine does not currently have any type of buoy or other marker that would be specifically used during loon nesting times on Maine lakes. They are working on developing some program, but nothing firm yet.

The state buoys were removed on the first weekend after the Fourth of July as the birds and babies had left the nest and were exploring other parts of the lake. The buoys were no longer needed. As for the newly engineered loon buoys the lake association now owns, they will be sealed and tested, and ready to go for next seasons, loon hatchlings.

You know, after a relaxing beverage and some quiet reflection, I had spent three days working to protect the feathered birds. And even before I had deployed the state buoys, they had vacated the nest. Was it an exercise in futility, or a look to the future in our care for the black and white birds that capture our attention and admiration? Me, I'll have another vodka and Coke and stop listening to public outcry.

Thought: *Failure is an orphan, but success has a thousand fathers.*

no clue

It was another warm sunny day on the shores of beautiful Bauneg Beg Lake. I can't remember ever experiencing such a weather pattern during the summer months like we had this year. Every weekend was sunny, warm, and without precipitation. The lake had sixty-nine pontoon boats tied to their docks around the lake along with countless other boats, jet skis, floating platforms, some with picnic tables. It was a banner year on the lake.

As was my typical day, I had done whatever chores that needed to be done in the coolness of the early morning. I needed the afternoon to rest, read, and imbibe. I mean... hydrate. After having lunch, I found myself sitting on the front deck overlooking the pristine waters of Patriot Cove, hydrating on vodka and Coke, and reading a trilogy, written by my friend and neighbor. While I was totally engrossed with the shenanigans of my little otherworldly heroin, I was brought back to the present by a noisy truck backing down the right of way. Now what?

The black pickup truck was backing a trailer with a jet ski, stopping at the water's edge. The three occupants got out and removed the tie-down straps from the machine, getting it ready to launch. I'd seen it a thousand times. Why did I think this time would be different? And yet, it was!

Once the straps were removed, the driver backed the truck into the shallow waters of the boat ramp, getting just enough water over the trailer so the other two men could bull the machine off the dry carpeted trailer bunks into the water with minimal effort. I had to take a drink from my tumbler. I was already getting tired watching them. Once they had the machine off the trailer, the driver pulled ahead but stayed on the ramp. The other two men turned the machine toward open water, but before getting the machine in deep enough water, started the jet ski. Having owned a 2006, 4-stroke, Sea-Doo, Bombardier, with a supercharger, I had a fair knowledge of these high-powered crotch rockets.

As soon as they started the machine in the shallow water, the jet pump sucked up dirt, gravel, rocks, and whatever debris lay on the bottom beneath the now dying machine. The area around the machine was turned into a cauldron of swirling mud. I knew instantly the machine would not operate like they thought it would. The debris was forced through the jet pump, out the rear housing, through a wear ring that protects the impeller, which provides all the thrust and speed for the machine. The wear ring is about the diameter of a dessert plate, 0.000025 inches thick, give or take a smidgen, but when scored by any debris, will fail to let the machine get up to speed or operate properly. No easy day! I stepped inside the cottage to replenish my beverage, knowing this show was not over.

When starting a machine correctly, it is only natural that the operator wants to jump on the crotch rocket, hit the throttle, and get out on the lake to terrorize the locals. Instead, this guy cranked the throttle to high speed and got a slow ride to nowhere. I could out-swim the machine. Not that I wanted to. For the next forty-five minutes, they removed the seat, fiddled with the plugs, wiring, checked the oil, and each time they thought they had the machine ready to go, the same thing would happen. High throttle and no acceleration. Just slow forward movement to nowhere. They finally decided to trailer the damaged machine and return to parts unknown. For now, I had witnessed the death of another high-powered jet ski, but was able to leave this reality behind and delve into another realm where my beverage would serve me well. Good luck guys!

Several days later, still engrossed in my trilogy on the deck over-looking the pristine waterfront, I again heard the noise of a truck backing a trailer down the right of way. It didn't take long to see it was the same truck, with the same jet ski, and the same three men, coming to launch their machine once again. Had they repaired it? I had my doubts, but anxiously awaited the results.

Putting the machine in the water, they again turned the machine toward the center of the lake and started the machine, this time in a little deeper water. It started... then stalled immediately. They went through that process over and over again. Finally, the machine started, stayed running, and the operator jumped on the seat, thinking once he gave it some throttle, he would fly out onto the lake. I could feel his disappointment when he went about five feet at high throttle only to get nowhere. He tried several more times to start and go, only to end up dead in the water. After managing to get the machine back to the beach, they removed the seat cover, and the three of them looked over the internals like three doctors getting ready for surgery.

With the seat cover off, the operator tried to take off from a standing position. I thought to myself, *Well, that's a dangerous thing to do. If the engine throws a piston or other parts, this could be an instant and painful colonoscopy.* While I felt bad for the guys, I was so hoping for more... well... action. Try as he might, the little jet ski would not go. It would not do anything but rev up and go nowhere. I could feel the disappointment from my perch. There was only one thing I could do. So, like a trooper, I went into the cottage and got a cold vodka and Coke. I felt better already... not so sure about the troops out there with a broken machine. They still had no clue. After another forty-five minutes, they took the machine out of the water and returned to parts unknown. Sorry guys... maybe next time.

Several days passed when again I heard a trailer bouncing down the right of way. Lo and behold, if it wasn't the three musketeers returning with their water rocket. This time, the machine was on the trailer facing backwards for some reason. I'm not even going to venture a guess. One of those things where you had to be there. So, anticipating another forty-five minute adventure, I sat on the deck and relaxed to take in the show. I hoped the third act was better than the first two.

Again, they put the machine in the water, started it, and went through the same useless exercise as the last two visits. As the machine started, they cranked the throttle to high rpms but only went five feet that an armless man could out-swim. Okay, that was a cruel analogy, but vodka will do that. For the next several minutes, the men looked under the seat, fiddled with whatever they fiddled with, started the machine with the cover off, anything they could think of to get the machine going more than 1 mph for ten seconds and ten feet away. The disappointment was palpable, even for me. It was time to do something I NEVER do. Go help them!

They were all standing around the machine with blank looks on their faces. I approached them and the conversation went like this:

Me: "Excuse me, do you know why you can't get the machine up to speed?"

Man: Looks at me like I have two heads. Says nothing.

Me: "Didn't you put this machine in here a week ago when you noticed it couldn't get up to speed?"

Man: "Yes."

Now we're getting somewhere!

Me: "When you came the first time, you started the machine in shallow water. The intake is like a high-powered vacuum cleaner and sucks up everything under it into the jet pump. You need to be at least in two-to-three feet of water to safely start these machines to avoid sucking up rock, sand, and debris. I heard it all from my house. What happened is, you blew the wear ring around the impeller. The only way to fix this is to replace the ring. Do you know what a wear ring is?"

Man: "What?"

Me: "The ring is a cylindrical piece of molded heavy plastic that fits tightly around the impeller housing in the jet section that gives it the thrust and speed you need. When you score or damage the ring with rocks and sand, the machine loses all its power to go forward. The ring is only about $50, but the repair in a shop goes for about $800."

Man: "Oh, we can replace it ourselves. That's no problem!"

Me: "Well, if you didn't know what a wear ring was, I doubt you can repair this machine. But, you should look at a YouTube video on how to do it before you rip off the rear end. It's the only way you'll get this machine to work. You need to replace that ring. It's only a three hour job if you know what you're doing. Probably not what you want to hear, but good luck with it."

I had done my part for the betterment of society. Another good deed done. I wonder now if I should have mentioned a special star wrench they would need to remove the impeller. They'll figure it out! Now where's my beverage? I think I left it on the deck rail!

outwitted

For the past twenty-seven years, six months, one week, six days, ten hours, and a few minutes, I've lived along the shores of beautiful Bauneg Beg Lake. The happy memories that have been made here are countless. Of course, I've recorded many of them in my previous ramblings. And yet these special times and events keep coming at me like movies at an all-night drive-in. Remember those? Me neither.

Living on a lake means living with Mother Nature and all her creatures. Maybe *living* isn't the right term; maybe more like *dealing* with the little vermin. Over the years, I've encountered deer, moose, Canadian geese, loons, hawks, turkey buzzards, eagles, mallard ducks, snakes, turtles, squirrels, chipmunks, moles, and mice. Had I known this years ago, I could have operated my own lake safari adventure business. While I think of myself as an animal friendly person, I do not approve of critters in my storage area (cellar) leaving their, well, *leavings* behind for me to find. When I least expect it, I'll come across leavings in my tool bin, under the grille cover, under the swing seat cover, and generally in any area the little crap factories decided they had the urge. No wonder I drink! I don't have the time to keep cleaning up after these unwanted guests. Not to mention that over the years, they have chewed through fabric and material items I had stored in the area, turning it all into unusable junk. Little heathens!

A few weeks ago, I'd had enough and thought I'd try to humanely rid myself of these little crap-leaving vermin. I went on Amazon (like who doesn't, right?) and found a couple of small Havahart traps to my liking. The time had come for me to rid the cellar of these little beasts who used my space as their personal toilet. They never even used toilet paper. How rude!

Anxious for my order to arrive, I was giddy with anticipation. As you can tell, I am retired and have little else to do. At my age, *giddy* is good though! Then one afternoon, unexpectedly, my phone trilled, letting me know my package had been delivered. I could hardly contain my excitement, knowing it was my turn to leave *them* an unwanted surprise. I opened the well-known Amazon box and found the two traps inside, just begging to be used.

I showed off my new deterrent machines to the wife, but she wasn't impressed. She's an animal lover and thinks rodents are cute. She hasn't seen the cellar!

After showing off my new finds, I went to work loading them up with peanut butter and real nuts. I placed one in the cellar pump room and one in the outside storage room. Then I waited for the next day to see what I would find. I hardly slept all night, listening for the cage door to snap shut. I could visualize the fear in the critters eyes. Payback was on my doorstep!

The next morning, I returned to the cellar, snapped on the lights, and approached the pump room door. I slowly opened the door to peer inside and found the trap door was shut. I had caught my first... mouse! He was a little guy and wasn't really happy to see me. He stayed on the farthest side of the small cage away from me as I carried it to the workshop. Now, my dilemma was... how do I get rid of it? Drowning at the dock seemed a little barbaric. Any other form of death seemed like torture. I didn't feel right *killing* the little guy. He was one of God's creatures, was he not? He had bulging brown eyes, a short pointy nose, and looked helpless against a much larger foe. I

17

was a *foe*? A guilt-ridden foe? Now what? I could have used a good vodka and Coke during those moments of indecision. I finally decided that I was not going to be the instrument of death. I opened the lid to my 55-gallon trash barrel and dumped the cage contents in it, leaving the little mouse to wander through the trash pile and eventually succumb to... well... his demise. I closed the lid tightly. At least he wouldn't be crapping in my cellar again. I loaded the cage one more time with fresh peanut butter and returned to the cellar and placed it where I knew it would do the most good. Maybe I had time for that drink after all.

After breakfast the next morning, I returned to the pump room to inspect my catch. I was not disappointed when I entered to find the cage door shut and another small mouse looking at me through terrified eyes. Two days, two mice. I was okay with that. I brought the cage back to the shed, and, like the day before, opened the 55-gallon trash can and relieved the cage of its diseased, bacteria infected contents. Another critter bites the dust.

I didn't have much trash in the plastic bag that lined the plastic barrel, so I prodded the trash with a stick but could not find any sign of the previous day's occupant. Thinking nothing of it, I saw the new little prisoner cowering in the bottom of the barrel, closed the lid tightly and reloaded the cage for more work. The cage outside the pump room had never tripped.

The next morning, I returned to the pump room to again find the cage door shut and another mouse inside looking at me with the same large brown eyes, snout nose and small tail. I was catching the whole family. I brought the cage back to the shed, and again emptied its contents into the larger receptacle. Looking down, I didn't see the previous day's occupant anywhere in the barrel... or the one before that.

I took a closer look at the barrel's interior and noticed some defects in the plastic bag's sides... like a little rodent crawled up the side and made its way out through a small crack in the barrel's cover. I was flummoxed! Bewildered! How could this be? I looked into the barrel but only saw the little mouse I had just put in there. I think he was smiling at me! There was no sign of the two previous days' occupants... or was there?

Was this the same critter I'd been catching day after day? Was it possible the little creature had outwitted me day after day? Was I drinking enough? I thought the little guy looked familiar. This time though, I had to make certain he was not the same captured rodent I thought he was. So, I took steps to make sure he would not escape the large round prison I was using. Then I loaded the cage for a fourth day in a row and returned it to the pump room. The waiting began!

The next day, I returned to the pump room again, slowly opening the door. Looking inside, the little cage was empty. The peanut butter and loose peanuts were still placed where I had left them. I closed the light and left the area. I went back into the pump room over the next several days and found nothing. I went back to the shed and looked inside the barrel to make sure the little critter was resting comfortably... he was. This meant only one thing. I had been outwitted by a 2-ounce mouse who ate my food, still crapped in my pump room, and faked being scared of me every day. Man, those little guys are smart. Me, well, I'll leave the cages loaded and not worry about how often they'll work. I have a book to read and a beverage to enjoy. Life is good on the shores of beautiful Bauneg Beg Lake!

taking the worst of it

It was a warm late summer afternoon, and a picture-perfect day for an evening cruise around the lake. The temperature was in the high 70s, and the loons were being cautious of our presence as we slowly sailed by them. Dusk was going to settle over the lake soon, so it was a perfect time to cruise the lake and enjoy its ambiance. All around us we could see twinkling lights from the nearby cottages and take in the smells of campfires people were enjoying.

Earlier in the day, we had gone to dinner with friends from out of town. It was our weekly routine to have dinner with them after attending local church services, then return to the small cottage and take an early evening cruise before returning to share dessert and coffee.

As was typical on these weekly rides, the ladies sat up front, each taking a seat. They had removed their shoes and brought their feet up under themselves for a restful and comfortable ride. The two guys sat across from each other, me in the captain's chair, and shared light chit chat about weekly grocery prices, the cost of Alaskan king crab, the price of Saudi oil, and a multitude of other world-saving issues.

We had just made the turn at the north end of the lake and were proceeding down the east side of the peninsula when our peaceful ride went south. (NO, not the boat!)

Out of nowhere, a single solitary little hornet, the size of a penny, started buzzing around the boat, unbeknownst to me, the boat captain. I was proudly wearing my Navy veteran ball cap and didn't even notice the little kamikaze striped flying bug in the area. But the friend's wife did, and from her perch on the front of the pontoon boat, she came rushing at me like a madwoman on steroids.

She had a cloth of some kind in her hand. I couldn't tell from the blur I was seeing. She started pelting me with it in rapid, successive blows. I was wondering what the heck was going on. She was in full assault mode, her arms flailing hither to and fro like a madwoman. Her heavy swats were hitting me in the head and shoulders area, making my hat spin on my head, and my glasses go askew (that's right... askew) on my now battered face. I couldn't stop the constant barrage of cloth whiplashing I was receiving. I had to shut off the boat engine because I couldn't see through the onslaught. Being a former Navy enlisted man and serving in the world's most powerful nuclear Navy, I had to weigh my options lest things got worse. The beating finally subsided, just before I was going to throw my assaulter over the rail. While her husband coaxed me to do just that, I found it would just be more work for all of us.

Me: "Hey, what the heck is wrong with you? You crazy or something?"

Her: "There was a hornet around your head, and I didn't want you to get bit."

Me: "And you thought beating the crap out of me was going to stop the hornet from biting me?"

Her: "I didn't know what else to do. I thought I'd save your life."

Husband: "Told you to throw her in the water. I can pick her up next week!"

Me: "Where's my hat, and who's going to straighten out these glasses? Did you at least kill the hornet?"

Her: "No, he got away, I guess. But you're safe now."

Me: "Not from you, lady. No coffee for you later, either."

21

In the meantime, the wife and my inner child were roaring with glee. I can't believe they're both against me now. The rest of the cruise was uneventful. Heck, we just went through an assault, so it couldn't get worse than that, could it? An hour later, the crazy woman went home, leaving me to wonder what ever happened to the little striped hornet.

I think next week I'll tell them I'm sick!

hillbilly fishing

There was a grayish mist overhanging the calm waters of the lake that late August morning. Looking out over the still water reminded me of what the moors in England might resemble on an early misty morning. And still, it was warm in the morning heat, looking to be another beautiful day on Bauneg Beg Lake. As was my morning routine, I had a cup of coffee in hand, looking out over my docking system and seeing all was well. The pontoon boat was floating calmly alongside its aluminum berth, some of the solar lights still twinkling in the early dawn. It was going to be another nice day.

Looking over to the left, something strange caught my eye alongside the wall belonging to The Botanists on Windy Way Point, near the boat ramp. It appeared like something out of a mystery movie. It looked like a flat-bottom, square-end dinghy tied up to the wall. It looked old and abandoned, floating there in the mist. With my curiosity piqued, I knew I had to walk over to take a closer look at the contraption I'd never seen here before. I checked my liquor cabinet before leaving the cottage to make sure I was ready for whatever this was.

Walking across the nearby property, I came up to the "trailer" that was used to haul the "dinghy" to the lake. It was parked near another neighbor's fence line. Whoever the unknown owners were, they made themselves at home, it seemed. The trailer was of homemade construction. It had two wheels under a frame whose bed was made of chrome wire shelving sections you would see at Walmart or other big box stores. The bed was held together with multiple zip ties, small diameter rope, and some wire. Yup, definitely homemade. The trailer tongue was the only thing that actually belonged to the trailer. Looking around the trailer, there was no registration plate and no lighting. Now I was bewildered. Where did this all come from? It wasn't here the night before. I walked over to take a look at the dinghy floating quietly nearby. Why am I hearing the dueling banjo song from the movie *Deliverance*?

If I thought the trailer was something to behold, the dinghy was a sight for a Saturday night horror movie. The 12-foot boat was dented and dirty inside and out. The decking had some five gallons of cloudy water with pieces of lake silt, fish parts, and mud floating in the bottom, along with a few beer cans and food wrappers strewn around. There was no motor and no oars. While these things aren't that unusual in themselves, let me tell you what was.

On the back of the boat, overhanging the edge, was a broken fishing pole. The top half of the pole was still connected by the fishing line, but hanging loosely in the boat. Protruding through the top of the pole was a fishing line which led to a 24-inch eel that was left dangling in the water. This was their bait, I guess. It was dead, half-eaten, and seemed to fit the entire scene. No, not done yet.

The boat was anchored by a clothesline which was attached to the boat cleat and the other end to a fluke anchor that was unceremoniously thrown up on the new lawn The Botanists had recently planted. It was stuck within feet of the much revered flagpole, gouging the green turf. I was glad The Botanists weren't here at the time. Not knowing any particulars of the situation, I was at a loss of what I might do, if anything. It was too early for vodka and Coke. So, I had to wait and see how this would pan out. The Botanists were not due back to their cottage for another few days, so I would keep an eye on all this to see what turned up. The game was afoot!

I left everything where it was and waited to see if the owner would come back. Nothing happened that whole day. By the following morning, they had struck again. The boat had been turned around, and the anchor was in a different location on the manicured lawn. The boat still had water and debris in the bottom, like the previous day. Still, no motor and no oars!

Finally, on the morning of the third day, the culprits had returned and were at the boat ramp. It took only a minute for me to get my clogs on and mosey on over to introduce myself to these two fishermen. They looked like they were in their late 20s, dressed in worn and scraggly loose-fitting clothes and worn sneakers. Neither had shaved in weeks or gotten a hair cut in months. They were good ole boys from Maine (I think).

Me: "Good morning, are you guys from around here?"

Them: "Not locally, but from Maine."

(They were both very polite. You can't be angry at polite people!)

Me: "Do you know this is a private way, and your boat is anchored on a private wall, and that your anchor is damaging private property?"

Them: "We're really sorry about that. We meant no harm. We'll get the boat out right now and we won't come back here."

After they loaded the boat, they walked up on the lawn and tried cleaning up the minor damage their anchor had made near the flagpole. The Botanists wouldn't even know they had been there.

Me: "I hope you're not going far. That trailer isn't going to take much rough road to fall apart. You have no plates or lights either."

With no response, they commenced to hook the makeshift trailer to their truck and remove the jon boat contraption from the water. They manually lifted the boat onto the trailer and tied it down with whatever rope they had. It was like a scene out of *The Ozarks*! (I'd love to see the Ozarks!!) Soon, they were traveling up Corbin Way to wherever they came from. Did I mention that despite their raggedy appearance, they were polite? I did?

Several days later, on a warm early afternoon, I heard another truck backing down the right of way with an 18-foot fiberglass bow rider with a 75 HP outboard motor. The boat was shiny, well kept, and sported Maine registration tags with the required milfoil sticker. But, more noticeable were the two men who put the boat in the water. It was the same two hillbilly guys that were here a few days before. What was going on? Did they trade in their beaten up dinghy for this late model boat with a high-end outboard? Once they launched the boat (from a new trailer), they parked the truck and trailer up the road out of the way of traffic while they went fishing. Later in the afternoon, they came back to the launch, easily loaded the boat on the trailer (with plates and lights), and drove off, never to be seen again. You can't make up this stuff.

God, I love this place!

best neighbor ever

I t was about a year ago that I got new neighbors. Our lakeside neighborhood didn't see too much turnover on this side of the lake, so it was refreshing to see a new family move in. About a week after the new couple settled in, I ran into the colonel, walking his little dog, Isabela, when we introduced ourselves. The colonel and the Mrs. were retired Air Force veterans living in a quiet compound in Melbourne, Florida. Why quiet? The entire 5,298 homes were all retired military, and fully armed with any assortment of guns (I mean, artillery) you could think of, along with hand grenades, flame throwers and a working Abram tank they disguised as a lawn ornament. Yeah, it was a *quiet* retirement compound.

After spending a very busy summer on beautiful Bauneg Beg Lake, the new neighbors had scheduled a late fall return to Florida. Snow, ice storms, Nor' easters, cold temperatures, and bone-chilling winds were not any of Mother Nature's gifts they were ready for. After three warm months of doing upgrades to the house, grounds maintenance, and new docks, they were ready to head south despite enjoying their time in Maine and making new friends. I was very pleased with the new neighbors and knew for sure we would become good friends. Before he left, the colonel gave me a key to his new digs in the event any emergency came up. Commuting from Florida for stuff was not high on his list. I felt honored that he trusted me. Of course, the place was rigged with security alarms, cameras, and the need to call him BEFORE I entered his domain so he could secure the alarm systems through a phone app. I guess he didn't trust Navy guys!

The day came when they packed their large, late model truck, and set out with their puppy, Isabela, southbound, headed for Florida. That same evening, I happened to look out over the right of way, when I noticed there were lights on in the colonel's house. *What was that about?* I thought to myself? I texted (I mean reported) the find immediately. I was told that in their zeal to leave, they may have left some lights on in the entryway area, and asked if I would go secure the lights. So, being the helpful neighbor, I walked over to the large house, using the new key with a New England Patriots logo, opened the deadbolt lock and let myself in. I secured the lights and made sure the space was secure before leaving. As is my custom, I secured the lock on the passage set, and then locked the dead bolt lock, giving the steel core door two levels of security. I left the area satisfied I had helped my neighbors, and texted them, so they could have a peaceful night's sleep, and could re-alarm the house against foreign intruders. All was peaceful on Bauneg Beg Lake.

Several months passed before I heard from the colonel again. Receiving a text, it seemed there was some issue at his house with the water system. While the water was secured at the source, his app told him there might be an issue. I was again asked to do some recon at the site and see what the hoopla was about. Donning my jacket and hat, I set off to see what was going on in the vacant house on the hill.

With key in hand, I unlocked the dead bolt, then went to unlock the passage set, only to find the key would not work. I tried several times, but to no avail. I tried one last time, but the key would only fit one lock. What was I to do? I went around the house trying other doors and looking for other ways that I might access the house, all with negative results. I now had a dilemma! Do I call the colonel, or go home and get a fresh vodka and Coke and mull it over some? I texted the colonel... first.

> Hey Colonel, I can't seem to get into your house. The key you gave me fits the dead bolt, but not the passage set. I locked both on the way out when I had gone to secure the cottage lights three months ago. Now I can't get in.

What's a passage set?

> The doorknob you use to access the house is the passage set, the upper lock in the dead bolt.

We never locked that knob. We weren't given any keys for it that I know of. The prior owners just handed us a bunch of keys and told us to figure out where everything went.

> Okay, so now what? Do you want me to call a local locksmith and get that lock opened before you get back?

No, I'll take care of it when I get back. I may have to break a small window or something.

> If you're sure. Maybe you do have a key in the bunch you got. In any case, I didn't see anything wrong at the house and couldn't hear any noises, so I think you're good, anyway.

Okay thanks, we'll talk later.

With that, winter rolled on without further incidents at their house. Good thing since I couldn't get in anyway. As spring came around, I reached out to the neighbors, knowing they were making plans to return to the lake house for the summer, their arrival only ten days away. The text conversation went like this:

Still good to come back to Maine locked out of your house? I can still get a locksmith to break in for you! LOL. Safe travels.

Hi, we'll be back on the 7th. Hopefully, we can get in… if not, I may need to borrow a hammer!!

Ok. Air Force, huh? Big hammer! See you soon. Been raining here for two weeks. Please bring the sun back with you.

Consider it done. Vol 2 out yet?

Manuscript done. Cover should be done this week coming. It's in design now. So, we're almost there. Jennifer is doing a super job. Smart lady. Book 3 is already being assembled. Got a lake trilogy going. Should I write a story about locking you out of your house? I can embellish some!

I'll bet you can… with enough vodka!

Sounds like he knows me.

Have a question… where did you get the carport for Jeannine's car? Billy finish the road yet?

The colonel can multi-task in conversation. In few words, he did his own recon in portable garages, the lake road repair, my books, and his locked house. No wonder I felt safe while he was on active duty!

The portable green garage is Jeannine's, and you can get one locally or online through Shelter Logic. The wood carport for my truck was built by my carpenter neighbor. The road is not finished. I called bobcat guy twice in as many weeks. Says he's on it. I can't push him too hard. He'll get it done soon.

Where locally? Did you set it up?

A small engine repair shop off Route 99. I think he'll get you the garage you need, but you have to pick it up. Then you, the botanist and I will have to put it up. You know... community service. Easy to do.

I no longer have a truck, hoping to find a beater truck to do dump runs, etc.

You can always use mine. It's here all the time.

Thanks, I may have to initially. Of course, we might have to sleep in it if we can't get into our house.

I'll get the back cleaned up and put some soft blankets in there for you. I suppose you'll want pillows?

What a kind gesture!

We're neighbors right? I sort of owe you a free night. You know, in case the hammer isn't big enough.

Is vodka included in this package?

For you it is. 80 or 100 proof? Any mixer or snacks?

Man... this is first class! I feel a story coming on.

Least I can do.

It would be a week before the neighbor's arrival. Would he have a right key to enter his lakeside domain? Would breaking and entering be forced on him? Time would tell. I was glad the neighbor had a sense of humor. Knowing he was armed to the teeth, I guess using a hammer to get into his house wasn't too much to ask. I will have a new bottle of vodka ready for his return, too! The least I can do!

Welcome back, neighbor!!

PS: When the neighbors returned to their lake house, the colonel did have a key that fit the passage set and was able to enter his summer domain without breaking into any windows. Another happy ending.

hard to believe

I t was late morning, and a very warm day on the shores of beautiful Bauneg Beg Lake. I had just finished mowing my lawn and getting the property looking as pristine as I could. Lately, the storms that passed through our area were growing in intensity, causing the 100-foot pines to shed their cones and needles by the truckload. I'm speaking from personal experience. So far, since spring, I had taken four full truckloads to the local landfill. I doubt I'm done. Is it due to climate change? I think so. Who knows for sure, right? Maybe Al Gore, our former Vice President and Nobel laureate who was awarded the prestigious medal for his work on climate change, was onto something. And yet... well, here we are. But I digress.

Trying to catch a few winks before taking on my next project, I was rudely awakened from my peaceful slumber by the sound of a truck backing a boat down the right of way. *Hey*, I thought, *it's only Monday, not the weekend when these boat specialists come down the 200-foot dirt road.* Yet, here they were. The truck backed down the road with some difficulty, trying to keep the trailer in the middle of the road in order to line up with the narrow ramp. Finally, within ten feet of the water, the truck stopped, and the two men got out.

Driver guy got out of the truck with a large cup of what looked like a Dunkin' Donuts coffee. Nothing says you're serious about boating unless you're holding a large cup of steaming coffee when launching your boat. Most folks have a beer, but coffee? Well, no matter. Getting out of the truck, he placed the large cup on the roof of his truck and proceeded to the back of the rig to loosen all the tie-down straps (I guess!!). He and passenger guy untied the bow straps, loosened some side ratchet straps and were ready to get the 18-foot bow rider in the shallow launch area. (I doubt they knew just how shallow the area was. Live and learn.)

Thinking they were ready, the driver got in the truck cab (forgetting his large steaming cup of coffee sitting precariously over his head), and started to slowly back the boat in the water. They had a fairly high trailer and they would have to back out quite a ways to float the boat off the trailer. He slowly backed in, and with the help of Passenger guy, they got the trailer deep enough that the boat should have floated off. But... no. Passenger guy (in the boat) rocked the boat from side to side with no results. Driver guy stepped out of the truck and came to help push the boat off the trailer, but still... no. Not one inch! Nada!

I thought it was funny that the coffee cup was still upright on the truck cab and that wisps of steam could be seen floating above the cup. How hot was this coffee? The guys decided to take the boat out of the water and check things over. Once back on the road, they found a strap at the back of the trailer that was still attached to the boat. Yeah, that might make a difference. Thinking they were now ready, they slowly backed into the water again, and still the coffee cup was staying put. Unbelievably. I thought I might yell out to them about the coffee. I didn't want anyone to get burned. Or worse, ruin a good cup of coffee. (They really should have brought beer.) I kept to myself like a good neighbor.

With the boat backed into the shallow area, both Driver and Passenger guy decided to pool resources and push on the front of the boat together. Finally, the trailer loosened its dry grip on the boat as it showed signs of movement, then it finally slid off the trailer and floated easily on the water. With a lanyard attached to the front of the boat, Passenger guy was able to maneuver the boat closer to the beach so he could get on.

There are many ways one can mount a floating boat. You can use the rear boarding ladder, or you can hoist yourself up from the side of the boat. Or you can jump on from the front... where the cleat is. Yeah, Passenger guy positioned himself in the front of the boat, and hoisted himself up in an acrobatic maneuver, twisting 180 degrees from facing the boat to facing forward. His intention was to land on the bow and swing his legs over to the seats. Got that so far? What he didn't plan on was landing his backside ON the cleat. His yelp was heard around the cove. I couldn't stop laughing. It had to hurt, but still... it was well... sphincter rattling funny! And here I was without a cold beverage.

Driver guy walked across the trailer tongue to see if Passenger guy was okay from trying to manage a self-colonoscopy. What was he planning on doing? However, as he walked across the trailer tongue, one foot in front of the other, he slipped and landed in the water, straddling the trailer. I wonder if he was planning on having any more kids. That had to hurt too! So one guy tried to give himself a colonoscopy, and the other a vasectomy. I should have gotten my cold beverage sooner. This was getting painful to watch, even for me. Although I wouldn't have changed anything. I still think they should have brought beer instead of coffee.

Finally getting the boat out in the bay, Passenger guy waved off Driver guy and yelled that he would meet him at the camp. So Driver guy pulled out of the water and, as he gained speed, the coffee cup came tumbling down the side of the truck, splashing Driver guy's arm with the now cooled off liquid. I'm surprised the cup stayed up there that long. While it got his attention, he didn't appear to get scalded. After the vasectomy try, coffee couldn't hurt him now.

Well, the boat had Connecticut stickers on it. Welcome to Maine and to Bauneg Beg Lake boys. Next time you come for a visit, you should consider bringing beer. See you on the water. Now, I'll have that cold beverage. That was a lot of work. I guess I should go pick up that coffee cup....

missed the class on seamanship

I was spending a quiet evening at home after a long day of pontoon riding and reading the exploits of my favorite sea captain, Juan Cabrillo and the crew of the Oregon, authored by my favorite action author, Clive Cussler. Did I ever mention I own ninety-six of his seafaring novels? On this particular evening I was in another world, dozing off to another Hallmark Christmas in July movie that The First Mate always enjoyed. It was about 8:45... Oops, I mean 20:45, when my iPhone pinged, alerting me to a call coming in. Who calls me at 20:45 in the evening?

Caller: "Hey Ron, this is Steve."

Me: "Hi Steve, what's up?"

Steve: "I'm out here on the lakebed when I came across a small boat floating out here with nobody on it. The boat is fully equipped with fishing gear and a trolling motor, but there's nobody on it. I'm worried that maybe someone fell overboard, and I'm not sure what to do."

Me: "First of all, I'll keep an eye out on Facebook. If anyone is missing, it will come up fast. Sounds more like the boat broke away from its dock and got away. I think you should latch on to it and get it to your beach for the night while we look for the owner."

Steve: "Okay, I can do that. Evelyn (his girl Friday) will post a picture on Facebook too!"

Me: "Okay, let's see what happens."

Minutes later my phone pinged again and a picture of the small 12-foot square ended dinghy appeared dressed in fishing rods, a trolling motor, and oars. Under the picture, I wrote that the boat had been rescued and was sitting at the northeast end of Patriot Cove. We were looking for the owner to come retrieve it. Within seconds, I received another ping on my busy phone, alerting me that someone I didn't know wanted to send me a message. So, I activated the Bat Signal and let the unknown messenger do just that... message me. The First Mate was getting a little agitated as this hallmark lake event was overshadowing her Hallmark Christmas movie. But I digress... as I often tend to do.

The message said, "Hi Ron, my name is Ophelia. The dinghy is ours! Thank you for keeping it safe. It must have busted loose this afternoon." To which I replied, "Just happy to hear you're safe and can get the boat back. It's safe for now." I went on to explain to Ophelia (how old is this woman??), that her prized fishing vessel would be safe overnight, that it was on the beach at the northeast end of the lake. She said she'd come get it first thing the next morning. With that, I returned for the final kissing scene under the Hallmark mistletoe. I think I'm getting weepy. I mean, two happy endings in less than thirty minutes.

The boat owners never made it the next morning like they thought they would. Sometimes the best laid plans never work out. It was early afternoon that my phone pinged with a most unusual request... from Ophelia.

OPHELIA
Would you call my husband at 617-555-8980?

(Not a real number)

Sure, but why?

He can't find his phone.

What kind of mess was I getting into? They can't tie their boat up securely, and now they can't find their phone. So, I called Mr. Ophelia, who answered his phone after several rings, and he got right into his dilemma.

Mr. O: "I'm down by the dam, and I can't seem to find my boat anywhere."

Me: "The boat is at the north end of the lake. You're in the south end. You need to come all the way to the north end. Do you know which way that is?"

Mr. O: "I'll have to teach my wife about where north is."

Me: "When you come out of the cove, turn left and come all the way up to the other end of the lake, look for a dock with two flagpoles and I'll meet you there and show you where your boat is."

Mr. O: "Okay, we'll paddle up that way."

After the strange phone exchange, some ten minutes passed and still, there was no sign of the boat owner. I decided to get on my 20-foot pontoon boat and go looking for the wayward dinghy crew. If they didn't know south from north, who knew where they were? After cruising around the south end, the only people I saw, or so I thought, were two women paddling a canoe with no urgency, coming north along the peninsula between the Crow's Nest and Green Wall Bay. I kept looking for Gilligan's crew but couldn't find them anywhere. I headed back to my perch on the deck to wait to see what might happen.

After twenty minutes, I noticed the canoe I had seen with the two occupants paddling easily in the warm sun coming up the middle of the lake between Windy Way Point and Poole's Point. As they paddled, they were observant, but kept paddling to the north end. I figured they were not the folks I was looking for because I told them about the dock with two flagpoles and I'd be there waiting for them. I then went to retrieve my 1943, Bu. Ships, Mark 28, Mod 0, coated optics, Navy Bridge Binoculars and took a closer look at the now still canoe. Then my phone pinged.

Mr: O: "Is this Ron?"

Me: "Yes, it is."

Mr. O: "I can't seem to find my boat anywhere. I've looked everywhere."

Me: "Would you be wearing an orange t-shirt in a canoe?"

Mr. O: "Yes, I am."

Me: "Turn your canoe around and look to your left, and you will see the dock with the two flagpoles I told you to look for. Do you see them?"

Mr. O: "Yes."

Me: "Paddle to the dock and I will meet you down there. I'll be waving my hat so you can find me."

He offered no response, but I saw the canoe turn in my direction and the two tired oarsmen started on their trek to my dock. As they got closer, I notice they were NOT two women as I previously thought, but two men. (My bad!)

As they approached the dock, and still some 80 feet away, Mr. Ophelia yells out, "Are you Ron?" I thought he was kidding, so I said, "No, Sheila... Yes, I'm Ron." I guess he was okay with that and asked where the boat was. I pointed up in the far corner of Patriot Cove in the exact location where the small fishing dinghy was securely beached. And off they went to retrieve the derelict little vessel.

Some fifteen minutes passed before they came into view again. Mr. O was paddling the canoe, and The First Mate had two large oars in the locks and was rowing the boat square end into the waves as they made their way south to their camp.

As they passed by, Mr. O yelled, "Thanks, again!"

I waved.

You know, I have to give them credit. It was a hot afternoon, and they paddled and rowed around Bauneg Beg Lake for hours. Kudo's to you guys for getting the job done. Are you thirsty? I have vodka and Coke.

sticky situation

W e became the proud owners of our little cottage in the spring of 1995. Since then, and it's inevitable, the lake goes through some sort of phenomenon each year that makes you scratch your head (or other parts), and has you wondering what the heck is going on. But each year I look for the next "biggest and greatest" Mother Nature event that keeps me "scratching stuff" on the beautiful shores of Bauneg Beg Lake.

We've witnessed strange events like walls of thick pollen floating treetop high across the lake, covering everything in its path with the green sticky powder. How many times have I cleaned the boat covers and deck furniture, washed my truck, and watered down my walkway so as not to bring the sticky crap in the house? There were many events involving flying insects that filled the cottage, reminiscent of a Steven King movie. And why does that have to happen at night? I had events that required some major demolition to get rid of a flying ant colony that numbered in the tens of thousands. We've been here when the 90-foot pine trees shed the pine needles to near ankle depth, and the following year shed their tree top pine cones that required plowing to clean the streets. I can't even count the trips to the landfill to get rid of all the debris. And over the years, we've been harassed by chipmunks, squirrels, and birds of every kind. (Darn you, Noah!) And yet, we go through the process of cleaning, gathering, raking, and dumping as we need to keep our Little Peace of Heaven as clean and comfortable as we can. You have to admit, it can be quite the chore.

This year, however, things took a more serious turn. The year boasted a record rain-filled summer season that saturated the ground to dangerous levels. More so if you live on the waterfront and tree roots are within a few feet of the waterline. The trees suck up the water, forcing the evolution of pine cones into large clusters in the treetops and heavy amounts of tree sap to run willy-nilly. The tops of the pine trees are reminiscent of Weeping Willows with large sticky, gooey pinecones sagging toward the ground. At some point, it all has to come down. Am I ready for the onslaught? Well, I have enough vodka and Coke, but I'm not sure about my energy.

This year, our phenomenon was the vast amount of sticky pitch that rained down from the pine trees on a daily basis. Not just a drop here or there, but a continuous down-pouring of the clear sap in biblical proportions. It was reminiscent of a biblical plague, for sure. The sap covered everything it rained on. Everything!

My deck canopy was covered. The deck furniture covers were saturated. The deck box was loaded so the green top looked white. The new 24-foot wood walkway I had just rebuilt was full of the glue-like substance as well as the aluminum dock itself. The boat covers were full. No matter where I went or what I touched, the sap was sticking to me. Taking it off was no easy task. At least not without a tremendous amount of patience and elbow grease, and whatever magic formula works. Is there one?

My truck hood was covered with the goo. It sat under the covered carport, yet the sap found its way on the windshield and hood. Really? The driveway and walkways were covered in pitch and you stuck to everything you touched and walked on. And everything stuck to the bottom of my shoes so I could track it through our house and leave sticky marks on the floor... you know, for my better half to clean up. That makes for a happy home right there. I mean, let the drinking begin. Maybe vodka takes off the pitch? That would be sacrilegious, and I'd lose a lot of friends if I did that. No, that isn't happening!

This situation has affected me personally. Why shouldn't it? I have no karma. I have an inner child that I don't get along with. I have a habit of falling a lot, though I never get hurt. So why should this new sticky issue not mess with me?

Recently, leaving the deck to go for a pontoon ride around the lake, I grabbed the rail and instantly got slimed with the sticky pitch. Now I had to go clean that off with rubbing alcohol and a rag. Going into the house to clean the goo, I noticed that whatever I stepped on was now stuck to the bottom of my flat-bottomed crocs. That's just great. After a few minutes, and talking in a foreign language, I was ready to go again. I wasn't touching those rails again either.

As I was walking on the wood walkway toward the boat, my croc shoe got stuck on the colorless pitch adhering to the walkway. My crocs were flat-bottomed, so the glue thought it would hold me fast to the deck. It did, and my foot came out of the croc, and with the next step, my sock was stuck in the pitch. Then I was barefoot! Are you kidding me? I retrieved my sock and croc, knowing more cleaning was coming. Maybe I should just throw out the socks! We managed to get the boat ride in, but wondered if I would get slimed by the sticky crap while I was underway. This stuff floats in the breeze. I think we need an exorcism!

One sunny afternoon, after doing some online research, I thought I'd try removing the stubborn sticky substance with rubbing alcohol. I had some 90% stuff and went to work rubbing it on the large plastic deck storage box. The cover looked like several birds had diarrhea on it. (Yuck, sorry!) I splashed some rubbing alcohol on the top and scrubbed it with a rag. It seemed the alcohol was breaking down the sap and removing it. Well, most of it. Two days later, it looked like I never did the work... again covered with pitch!

Days later, the time came for me to clean up the property of debris left behind by a recent windstorm. The grounds had a good smattering of twigs, small branches, and plenty of gooey pine cones. I spent two hours picking up three wheelbarrows full of the stuff. Although I was using manly work gloves, everything I touched stuck to them. Needing a break, I went into the house only to be stopped by She-Who-Must-Be-Obeyed.

"You can't go in the house with those shoes. Look at them." Looking down, I had pine needles and small twigs sticking out all around the rubber soles. The entryway carpet was full of debris, some of it pine sap. What a mess! So, I removed the offending shoes and cleaned them the best I could before going back out to finish the clean-up job.

Until I can figure out how to best tackle this issue, I have to live with it like all my neighbors on the lake. Mother Nature sure has a sense of humor at times. (Why am I not laughing?)

I wondered how this would end. What kind of mean-spirited event had Mother Nature thrown at us this time? What would it take to get all this cleaning done? At the very least, I was looking at re-staining the main deck and stairway next spring. I was bewildered about how best to clean the furniture and boat covers. I could see myself experimenting with everything and anything to make the unsightly, sticky, messy goo go away. Even my inner child was quiet.

Gee, that might be a benefit right there!

saved

I t was a cool fall day on the shores of beautiful Bauneg Beg Lake. I had called the marina to pick up the pontoon boat, ready to call it a year, but had no reply as yet. We hadn't used the boat as much as in previous seasons due to the high amount of rainfall we endured from Mother Nature this year. From Memorial Day to Labor Day, we had not gotten five consecutive days without some rainfall coming our way. The ground was heavily saturated with water and the lake level was abnormally high for this time of year. And yet, it was still our Little Piece of Heaven. With the boat tied steadfastly to the dock, it seemed a good time to get out on the water and cruise the lake in the warm but breezy morning. How many more days would I have this season?

With The First Mate in tow, we uncovered the boat seats and commented about the stiff northerly breeze that was snapping at our flags flying above the docks. Being a former mariner in the world's most powerful nuclear Navy, the stiff breeze had no effect on my boat handling prowess. If I could (and did) get my helmsman license to drive an aircraft carrier, this was child's play. But I digress! I do that a lot! Where was I going here? Oh, yeah!

We headed north into the wind, glad I had brought my spring

jacket. The boat handled fine, but was being blown sideways in the strong breeze. The canopy was up, which didn't help matters. As soon as I turned south along the peninsula, the breeze then shifted to the stern, and the ride became calm and much warmer.

We proceeded down the east side of the peninsula and soon noticed that the navigational buoys at Poole's Point had been removed the prior weekend, a sure sign that fall was coming to the lake. Staying clear of the shoal areas, we continued on past Kern Island and headed into Green Wall Bay, featuring the home of Mr. Hall of Famer himself, and his lovely bride, The Quilter.

Cruising by the Bay in the stiff breeze, we noticed something amiss. The owner's large 96 square-foot dark colored pontoon boat had broken free of the rear boat cleat and was bouncing dangerously close to the rock wall at the property's edge. Not sure if the boat was in the rocks yet, we decided to make a run to the dock and see if we could salvage the vessel from any damage. The canopy was up on the unhinged vessel, which would make it more difficult to maneuver. The First Mate and I got into 'salvage mode' and made for the right side of the aluminum dock.

Approaching the dock was easy as the bay provided some protection from the winds by the hilly terrain the house sat on. After tying up our pontoon boat to the dock posts, we started in on getting the derelict boat back to the safety of the dock. With the wind still billowing the canopy, it made the work much harder. I decided not to lower the canopy and tried to move the boat the 15 feet we needed to get it back to the safety of the dock.

Using a multi-colored braided nylon line, I managed to get myself on the wayward vessel, taking one end of the rope with me. I secured the rope using a figure-eight knot around the boat's upper rear rail. The First Mate handled the opposite end, and when I had secured my end of the rope, she began to skillfully pull the rear of the platform boat safely toward the dock. Once it got close enough, I was able to reattach the stainless steel snap hook to the boat's rear cleat. After a careful inspection, the boat was again made fast to the dock, and all was shipshape once again. All this salvage work was making me thirsty.

The winds picked up just as we were backing out of Green Wall Bay and were pushing us south in the process. While it wasn't unusual for us to go on morning expeditions with the boat, it seemed that today there was a reason. The day was *saved*.

This is Bauneg Beg Lake. It's what we do! Ahoy, lake neighbors!

chippy and the ghost snake

I t was a cloudy but warm morning at the little cottage on the lake. Or, as the locals called it in 1798, Bawnkneebegglayke. Yes, they were drinking grog provided to them by the early settlers who came from England and Spain because of the poorly run governments there. It didn't take long for our early ancestors to start making beer and trading it to the locals for furs, trapping equipment, and hunting materials that soon became known as Kittery Trading Post. As you can see, the beer made the locals slur their words, which were normally hard to understand to begin with. But as time went by, the locals and early settlers managed to keep making beer, increasing high prices at the trading post, and ruining the government here. Soon, the settlers wanted to go back to England and Spain, and the locals had started GoFundMe pages to help them. God, I love this place. But I digress as I have a tendency to do.

On one recent early morning, I stepped out the back door to check on the temperature outside and get a feel for what kind of day we were in for. The sun was rising in the azure blue sky, and there was a light breeze coming in from the north. Overlooking the mulch covered grounds, all looked well despite a scattering of twigs, pinecones, leaves, and other debris the trees felt obligated to disperse on my little piece of heaven.

As I was scanning the property, my eyes caught on something irregular near the septic tank area, where I noticed a hole about two inches in diameter. Going over to inspect the tripping hazard, I saw it was the entrance hole of Chippy, an old nemesis from days gone by. The little furry monster and I had issues in the past, with him coming out as the winner. Seems he was back. I had also found a second hole some 20 feet away that he was using to tunnel his way across the yard, sight unseen. The hackles on my neck immediately went up, and my inner child started taunting me.

Again, Chippy didn't ask for permission to tunnel the property. He didn't have a building permit as required by Code Enforcement, he didn't even ask me for an easement. How rude! And I wasn't permitted to have any type of apartment on the property without zoning board of appeals permission. What was Chippy thinking? It was time for an eviction notice! My inner child started to giggle. (Go away, darn you!)

Not sure how far along old Chippy was into the construction, so I started small by filling in the holes with the dirt and mulch he had removed, using my sneakered foot. Tamp, tamp, tamp, and that should seal the hole for some time. (Me, 240 pounds. Him, 2 ounces.) I knew better, though.

Later that same morning, I went outside and looked at the area I had buried hours earlier only to find the hole opened up and a little wider. I knew from the past that Chippy was not a pushover. Once he'd set his little pea brain on something, he was going to follow through. I walked over, peered into his domain and again packed the hole with the removed dirt and again tamped the area harder than before. To get his attention, I again covered up the second hole some 20 feet away. I was hoping he got the message... no vagrants (or varmints) wanted here!

The next morning, both holes were fully open and two inches wider than before. Seems Chippy was sending me a message. As I was looking around, I noticed a few piles of dog poo in the lot next door. *Well,* I thought, *I have a surprise for you, my little furry friend.* I went to get a shovel and picked up as much of the day old excrement as I could and returned to the site dumping the entire shovel full of crap in the hole. I backed it up with the dirt he had excavated, and tamped it all in, feeling pretty certain he would find this tactic pretty crappy. (Pun intended).

Feeling pleased, I left the area to await his response.

Later that day, I went outside to get the mail, and I was more than surprised at what I was looking at. Chippy had re-excavated the hole to a four-inch width, used the dog doo-doo as fertilizer to feed the green pine boughs and pine cones he used to decorate the entrance of the hole. The war was escalating. I hadn't even started watching the Hallmark Christmas movies, and this little turd was decorating for the holidays on my property without a permit.

The next step was to block both entrances with large stones, heavy bark mulch, and anything short of bricks that would deter Chippy from settling in. And like before, no matter what I did, Chippy would undo everything and continue to create his home for the winter. He was gathering fallen acorns and other tasty chipmunk food for the coming cold season and delivering them into the tunnel he'd created. It looked like a lost cause, so again, I had to bow to the victor of another lost battle. Nothing I did deterred the little beast. I was defeated... again. But I didn't lose heart. I had my trusty vodka and Coke to brighten the cold days ahead. If Chippy puts out a Christmas Wreath with lights on it, I'll be doing a GoFundMe page too! Here's to you, Chippy. Don't get your nuts crushed!

A couple of days later, I thought it was about time for me to get on with the laborious task of cleaning the boat cushions. Over the long rainy summer, and passengers with too much suntan lotion, the faux leather upholstery was showing signs of dark stains. It was a nice day, and I was in the mood to kill something, so stains it was. I got my trusty five-gallon bucket, some nuclear strength hand cleaner and some scrubby doo-hickies and went to work. After about thirty minutes of hard scrubbing and making some decent headway, I found I was getting mighty thirsty. It was time to call it a day and get the rest done in a day or two, or maybe next spring. I'm retired and saw no need to hurry it along, heck the stains will still be there in the spring, right?

While I was cleaning the last cushion with clean water, I glanced over the side of the boat and caught a squiggly line moving on the bottom about two feet from the pontoon and moving toward to boat. The water was about 18.58643 inches deep, and, looking closer, I saw what appeared to be a snake moving along the lake bed at a slow speed. I could see the head clearly and the snake was traveling along in the typical "s" formation you would normally see a snake move. It was about 3 feet long and was moving rhythmically along, seemingly unbothered by its proximity to the boat. I thought about going to get a stick or something and fish it out of the water, you know, to protect the women and children. Did I mention the snake was white?

This was an unbelievable, Bauneg Beg Lake, albino lake snake for sure. I found a long stick and tried tempting the snake to climb on, but it didn't do anything. It just stayed there and kept slithering at a slow pace ever closer to the boat. *What's going on here?* I said to myself.

It finally dawned on me that this was not what it appeared to be. Looking around, I looked up and here was my Ghost Snake. The apparition was in fact a jet flying at 8,000 feet and the jet and its vapor trail was being reflected perfectly near the boat. The long wiggly tail was actually rippling in the water, causing the effect. The head of the snake was the jet itself. This was a perfect combination of weird crap that could only happen to me. Yep, no karma and an inner child that hates me.

You know, you can't make up this stuff. It's what makes Bauneg Beg Lake so darn special.

the book signing

As I was waiting in anticipation for my first ever book signing, I reminisced on the road that got me to this point. I was in a satisfied, happy place, having written and published, not one, but four books about living here on the shores of my beautiful southern Maine Lake. All in one year. Over the many years, the lake has been described as "our little piece of heaven" by many, and it lived up to its reputation.

During the past twenty years, I had written more than 160 true short stories about life on the lake that I had personally witnessed. The stories ranged from personal stories, to stories involving my many friends here on the lake, using their lake monikers, stories of many four-footed animals of all weights and sizes, as well and those that take flight, and many stories of Mother Nature's fickleness in doling out New England weather all through the year. The most enjoyable tales I penned were of the people who visit or live here and never once failed to entertain and astound me in their humorous faux pas, and discombobulated shenanigans. Best neighbors ever. And they still are, despite my attempt to make them famous in my published rantings.

Last year (2022), as I was shoveling my driveway, my neighbor from up the street walked by with her big dog, Tuki. Or maybe he was walking her? Most people walk by and you get the customary, "How you doing?" Not this lady. I soon found myself in a meaningful conversation with a neighbor I hardly knew existed. She was friendly, personable, and spoke easily, like we'd been friends for years. I asked her what she did for a living since she was home every day. She stated that she was an author. I asked her about her books and she told me about her special genre of books in Christian Fantasy. I never met an author before, never mind having one live across the street. She had heard that I dabbled in writing short embellished stories, some with a smattering of sarcasm about the lake, and told me she'd be interested in reading some of the stories. Not sure how I felt about that, but all the lake folks I had written about read them, so I thought, *why not*?

A couple of days later, Jennifer (her real name: maybe I should give her a moniker too!) came by again with her pooch in tow, and I handed her three of the small booklets I had self-printed in a local copy shop. She took them home to read, and time went by before I saw her again. As she left, I kidded her, saying they would make good bathroom reading. She laughed as she went up the street with Tuki pulling her toward home.

In January 2023, I had seen Jennifer again. She told me she had read the stories, and said,

Jennifer: "You should consider publishing these stories."

Me: "Yeah. I don't think so. I just write for fun and only for the lake friends I write about."

Jennifer: "These are really funny and good to read. You write like you talk, and that's really good in storytelling. It's like you talk to the audience while you're telling the story."

Me: "I don't know, I never gave that much thought. I wouldn't even know how to go about getting started."

Jennifer: "I can help you through all of that. It's no big deal. I do it for my books."

Me: "I'll have to think about it and get back to you, but I'm not certain or confidant that I want to publish these stories."

Every time I saw Jennifer, maybe once I week, she would ask if I had made up my mind about getting my feet wet. I kept responding in the negative. What was keeping me? I could afford the project, and Jeannine gave me the go ahead, yet I was uncertain. Writing for my family and lake friends and neighbors was one thing, but getting my stories out in public was something else.

A month or two went by and her offer was constantly on my mind. I had talked to Jeannine often about the possibility of publishing these lake stories, but never coming to any decision. I wasn't sure what to do, and I was no computer wizard, so there was that. I prayed over it. I figured if God allowed me to write these stories, maybe He sent Jennifer to help push me along to publish them. Maybe it was time. Just maybe, but I needed more time to think about it, and more prayer.

One day, I was outside shoveling light snow when Jennifer came by and asked me if I was ready to jump in and get the stories published. She was willing to help me. I had no reason not to accept her more than a generous offer. I wasn't as reluctant as I was previously, so I finally caved and said, "Yes." I had no idea what I was getting into, and I was moving ahead on blind faith alone.

Within the week, she had contacted me about setting up my accounts so I could get my ISBN numbers (International Standard Book Number) and contact the book cover designers for my first cover. I had selected forty short stories, taken in no particular written order as my first manuscript. Working online, I had contacted both companies she tasked me with, and within minutes of doing so, I forgot that I had just recently changed my email address (due to constant hacking) and gave them both the wrong email address. There was no way they could get in touch with me now, and I didn't know how to fix this. My faux pas sent me into an immediate stress attack. "That's it. I'm done. I'm not doing this."

I contacted Jennifer and told her what had happened and that I was not going to go forward with the project. It wasn't worth it. I saw her again the next day (I had cooled down by then), and she had taken it all in stride. She had a calming manner and told me, "It's no big deal and I can fix all this in no time. I think you should reconsider and keep moving ahead."

I hesitantly agreed. I felt bad because I was not typically a stressed person. Where was all this coming from? Her calming demeanor set me back on the right track. After talking me off the cliff, she actually agreed to take on the project completely as my book manager. From that point on, she dealt with everyone without my involvement unless she needed my input. I was blessed! I paid the bills, and she did all the work like it was her own. She always said, "The hard work is done. You wrote the stories. Now, we just need to get them published." She made it sound easy, but I knew it was a lot of work for her, even as she was in the midst of writing her own novels.

Soon, I was back on track and moving forward toward the first book, *Living the Life on Bauneg Beg Lake*. It came out on Jeannine's birthday, March 29th.

When I received my first proof book, I was thrilled. The cover was beautiful and the book layout was as we had formatted it. I had no clue what a proof book was for. After receiving my first ever matte covered book, I thought it was perfect, and I let Jennifer move ahead with little to no changes. Little did I know that I should have taken the time to reread and edit the book carefully so we could upload any changes BEFORE we set it free for purchase. It was too late after I announced to the world that the book was available on Amazon. The book had several (two pages) required changes that got by me. This was my responsibility to do, and it got by me. I handled the other three books much differently. Hey, live and learn, right? Once I understood more clearly what I should have done, I sent the corrections to Jennifer, who uploaded the changes, making the book read like a third grader didn't write it. To make things right, I sent a notice out to all the folks I was normally in contact with to tell them of my premature book release. I offered them a new, updated version for free. Only one person asked for a corrected copy. And she was an English teacher, so it goes to show. Several folks chimed in that they were happy with the proof version and wanted to keep it.

As the months went by, Jennifer and I published the trilogy of *Living the Life on Bauneg Beg Lake*. Book 2 came out at the end of May, and Book 3 came out on September 1st. I was very happy with those two well-edited books. Jennifer provided some editing as well as we went forward. While she worked all year on my lake stories, she was publishing her own fantasy novels in her *Ariboslia* trilogy and working on the *Cursed Lands* trilogy. She was amazing at the level of work she could manage, all with a smile on her face.

Book four was different. It would be a testament to my friend, dubbed The Lake Mayor. It was a title he earned because of his outgoing, friendly attitude and his willingness to help anyone in need without question. So, Jennifer was tested with more photos, more formatting and she even provided much more time editing on this issue that went along with her other work in getting this special issue done on time. And she did just that. I had asked for a release date on December 1st, and she uploaded the live copy on Amazon on November 30th. Oftentimes I refer to her as a Rock Star, because she really is. God wouldn't send anyone less.

I had been approached in the past by several people to have a book signing session. See, I'm getting to the meat of the title. I never thought I'd need to, since I was signing so many at the lake meetings in May and July. What was the point? However, since those two meetings, I had two other books available and folks were buying them. I thought maybe they'd like the opportunity to have them signed before Christmas should they be given as gifts. So, I published on Facebook and through email that I was setting aside two days for a book signing event. Or BSE for short. Yeah, not a real thing. I set aside December 16th and the 23rd from 12 noon to 3 p.m. for folks to come to the house and get their books autographed. I even mentioned that I had extra copies of all four books should folks want to get the set before Christmas, foregoing ordering, and shipping charges.

The night before the big day, I took my shower and used twice as much hand soap so I wouldn't have that old fart smell us elderly folks sometime exude. I don't, but why take chances? I groomed myself to perfection, ready to meet my peeps. The next day, I cleaned the house, and turned on the Christmas lights in the entryway and the house. It was warm, cozy, and inviting. Damn Central Maine Power, I was ready to party with my audience. Soon, the noon time hour came, and I opened the kitchen door for people to feel welcomed, thankful for the mild weather and sunny day. I sat at the kitchen table with my extra books and waited for the first autograph seeker to arrive. While waiting, I entertained myself by reading Jennifer's third book, *Aloft* in the *Ariboslia* series.

By 12:30, no one came. I got up and looked out the back door to the driveway, envisioning cars waiting in line. But only my lonely truck could be seen. At 1 p.m., I went to look again, and saw that the mailman had come, so I went to get the mail and my three Christmas cards that were delivered.

By 2:30, there was still no activity in the small cottage. I was smiling to myself, thinking in the back of my mind that there would be no book signing after all. I was not in the least disappointed or hurt. While my original plan was to publish these works as a legacy for the family, this is truly what it was ending up being. At 3 p.m., I closed the door, shut off all the Christmas lights until early evening, and returned to my normal everyday activity. I got a cold beverage, settled in my Lazy Boy and fell asleep watching TV.

God, I love it so!

PS: Next week I will do it all again, and I doubt anyone shows up! God is good!

the outage

C hristmas was two weeks away when the weather prognosticators started their daily vigil tracking a large storm that would form in the south and travel up the eastern seaboard, bringing heavy rain and damaging winds. At the time, neither storm had morphed into anything more than clouds and a breeze. How could they tell of this impending doom heading our way?

As the days passed, the weather forecast conditions were getting more dismal. When the storm drew closer to the shores of the lake, it gave me pause. Was I ready with all my normal foul weather preparations? Would the generator work if I needed it? Did I need to bring my rain gear in the house ready for use? Was it too early to be seen outside wearing my 9-inch L.L. Bean boots? And the biggest concern looming before me was, did I have enough vodka and Coke to ride out the coming storm? Of course, the answers to all these important questions was, yes! I tried to relax, but the constant worsening weather reports elevated my stress levels. That can't be good, right?

The day before the storm was to hit, the weather was calm, partly sunny, and the temperature was hovering in the mid 40s. That morning, I had noticed that the water level on the lake bed had dropped some two feet from where the water lapped the shore two days earlier, a certain sign that this would be a "Storm of the Century." Luckily, the storm would begin in the wee hours of the morning and ramp up during the following day. At least I'd be awake for the worse part of the storm. Besides, I don't drink much after 9 p.m., regardless of any circumstances. Must be the effects of old age.

Pleased that I had taken all the proper precautions for the coming storm, I went to bed at my usual time and slept soundly until about 3 a.m. when the winds started blowing and I awoke to the rain pelting against the bedroom window. I got up about 5:30 a.m. and got ready to face whatever the day would bring. The winds had already gotten stronger, and that always made me nervous living under skinny 90-foot tall pine trees. The trees were old, rotting from previous storm damage, and this year, their tops were brimming with thousands of pine cones stretched across the canopy like a wide brimmed Easter bonnet. Yeah, I was up early.

The rain was coming down very hard, and the winds were ramping up in intensity. It was about 8:30 a.m. when the strongest wind gust of the day came through the lake and Patriot Cove. Being a nautical person, and having done my share of ocean meteorology, I guesstimated that the gust came through at about 60 to 65 mph. And because it was concentrated on a narrow path, it was a damaging gust. The windows shook in the small cottage. What lasted less than 10 seconds seemed like an eternity. Normally, the winds blow from west to east, but this storm was in reverse. The winds came from the east and gusted inland off the ocean. No, that wasn't good! The only good thing was that the temperature was in the mid 50s.

After that gust came through, I went into the entryway of the cottage to see what damage I might find. I hadn't heard any large tree fall, so that was good. Looking out toward the street, I saw the wife's green portable garage (10 ft. x 20 ft.) had broken loose at the entrance area and the structure was bouncing up and down, slamming itself into the hot top area as the winds ballooned the tent, trying to rip it completely out of the ground. It actually resembled a hot-air balloon. I had the garage deeply anchored in six areas that should have been nearly (but not so) impossible to break free. I watched in fascination, no less, as the front 10 feet kept lifting and bouncing like a kangaroo on steroids. Good analogy? And our newest vehicle was parked in there. That vodka and coke was looking good right then, you know, to help calm my nerves, and steel myself to get out there and stop the madness. The tent was moving like Auntie Em's house in the Wizard of Oz. But this wasn't Kansas, Dorothy!

At about the same time, or about 8:37 and 43.869 seconds, the power went out, and we lost all contact with the outside world. It was time to man-up, get dressed and get outside. With no generator, there's no potty. Can't have that with a storm like this. So, I got my L.L. Bean boots on and went out to start the generator.

Once I got into the entryway, I found my rain pants and jacket where I had left them the night before. I sat in the chair to get my rain pants on. I'm a somewhat portly guy and lifting my legs into things, at seventy-four years old, is sometimes trying. I looked at the rain pants, and made certain the bib area was pointing in the right direction, then I slipped my right booted foot into the large opening. Trying to get my left leg in proved to be quite the challenge. After a few vain attempts, and my patience rapidly waning, I looked down to see what the issue was. I had put my right leg into the left leg of the yellow pants, making it impossible to get them on. It wouldn't have been so bad had my inner child not started goading me. What is wrong with her?

Removing the pants, I was already breathing heavy and not happy. Of course, wearing rubber boots with a rubber rain outfit seems self-defeating. If you know me... never mind. I finally got the pants off, aimed the bib forward and tried putting on the pants again. I got them on the right feet and I stood up to cinch the shoulder straps in place so I could get to work. Once on my feet, I was fumbling around, looking for those white shoulder straps. I found one and yanked it up over my shoulder, only to come to a screeching halt. While putting on the pants, one strap fell inside the pants, between my legs, and was now giving me a sharp wedgie, halting any progress on getting the pants on. Before my voice changed octaves, I again removed the pants. Now I'm breathing heavy, my glasses are steaming up, I'm already tired, and I think that stupid inner child is going to wet herself. She better be wearing Depends.

I sat down, and again, huffing and puffing and talking to myself, I took off the pants. What else could go wrong? I took a deep breath to gather my self-respect, and once again, slowly tried to put the rubbery rain gear back on. I took my time, made sure I had the right leg in the right place and that both straps were on the outside of the pants. I finally stood up, ready to put on my rain jacket. Oh no! I had put the pants on backwards and the stupid bib was now in the back. My inner child was roaring with glee. Why does she have to be like that? I was completely zoned out. I screamed at the top of my lungs for several seconds. The wife came out to the entrance area to calm me down and help me yank the pants off, and then it happened. I tore the back of the pants almost the whole length of the garment. All that time and effort, and there would be no rain pants today. Where is my vodka? I'm drinking it straight.

After I gathered what was left of my dignity, I decided to wear the pants anyway since the rain was coming down so hard, figuring any protection was better than nothing. I just tucked the ripped flap in my back pocket. It stayed two seconds and just continued to flop around like a watered down Band-Aid. I went to start the generator, and it ran great. I flipped the electrical switch on the side of the house from CMP to Generator and looked inside the bay window for the kitchen light. Nothing. Now what? The generator was humming along nicely, the switches were all in the right position, but no power was getting into the house. First, I checked the wired cable to the machine. It was inserted properly and locked. The box on the house was low to the ground, so I had to lie down on the slanted wet brick walkway to check the connection I couldn't see. I removed and rein-serted the cable and finally got it locked in properly. Finally, the house was powered. Good thing too, because I really had to go potty! I'd had a hard morning so far.

It was difficult for me to get off the wet ground since I had weak knees. I was close to the house, so I placed one hand on the electrical box and pushed off the ground with the other hand. Not looking at the ground, my weight was already pushing me up when I felt the pain of a pine cone being crushed by my hand. Once I got up, I had to peel off the imbedded pine slivers. My hand looked like the dents on a golf ball. What else could go wrong?

I walked down the driveway to the garage that was shaking and banging like it needed an exorcism. The wind had torn out two of the six in-ground cable anchors and shredded several bungee cords that were holding down the frame and the cover. The front end was still bouncing up and down as I tried to take hold of it. The wind was ballooning the tent and had moved the front of the structure some three feet over into the main driveway, bending the metal frame with it. It was a useless effort against such a strong wind. It didn't stop me from speaking in tongues, although I had no idea what that gibberish was.

I took one of the uprooted anchor cables and wrapped in around the lower structure frame and re-anchored the garage in the ground the best I could. I had two 12-inch long steel spikes and drove the cable into the ground. The wind was settling some, and my new improvised anchor seemed to steady the whole garage. For now, I just didn't want to lose the whole thing to my front lawn or wrap it around a tree. Once it was fairly stable, I moved the GMC to my neighbor's driveway for safe keeping. There were no trees there.

Looking over the property, the area was strewn with tree debris, broken limbs, and pinecones. It would all have to wait until the spring cleanup. Having my immediate issues taken care of, I marched up the street to assist Mrs. Mayor in starting her generator.

I got there and opened up the little shed that housed the unit. I tried to start it using the push button, only to find the battery was dead. I returned home to get my small portable power pack and went back up the street. I hooked up the terminals and switched on my little power unit. The generator sucked up the electrical charge but still didn't have enough energy to start. I stopped in to tell Mrs. Mayor about my dilemma, and that I'd be back in two hours after I recharged my power unit. Luckily, it wasn't cold out. Good fortune came my way about thirty minutes later. It seems Mrs. Mayor's son-in-law found the manual pull cord on the generator and got the machine started. She was happy, and I was happier. I was home and ready to ride out the rest of the storm. More good news, the phones were working.

I was barely out of my ripped rain pants when I received a text. Another friend up the street needed help to start their seldom used generator. So, I put on my rain pants once again and trudged up the street. When I arrived, the folks were in the garage looking over the small generator, willing it to start. Yeah, it doesn't work that way. However, I was there to help salvage the situation. I didn't do that well at Mrs. Mayor's house, but still. So I commenced to ask questions like I knew what I was doing. You know, how's your cat doing? Do I smell chili? I finally got down to business and gave the small generator a once over inspection. The gas was on, the starter switch was on, but the fuel was older than Methuselah. So, I pulled the starter cord several times and couldn't even get compression. However, because there were three of us standing there willing it to start, Mrs. Author's husband yanked the cord hard several times, making the generator cough and spurt, and finally it roared to life. Soon they had power going to their home, and all was well in their realm. Me, I walked home, tucking the long yellow flap from my ripped rain pants in my jeans back pocket. Lasted two seconds, so I just let it drag on the ground on the way home. What a morning!

Hardly in the door in my warm cottage, when I heard a knock on the door. It was another neighbor who had a problem starting her generator. Really? What the heck was going on here?

So, I donned all my gear and went out into the pouring rain once again. At least this time, the issue was only 50 feet away. The neighbor had a very small and very old generator. I had seen her husband (currently absent) start this unit before. He used to jiggle the choke, spray starter fluid in the air breather, run around the machine three times, utter some chant to the generator gods, then pull the starter cord hoping the old thin chord wouldn't break inside the rusted housing. What was I expected to do? I wasn't very successful at the other two places I'd been at, and this thing was worse.

We ended up calling her husband, and he tried walking me through the steps to persuade the little generator to start. Try as I might, the little power unit that once could... couldn't and didn't. It would have to wait until later when he could come and perform his rituals to coax the machine to start. Hours later, he was outside with a tool kit and had disassembled half the machine in some effort to start it. I went back out to help... what is wrong with me? I took the carbon laden spark plug he'd removed to my workshop and cleaned it up with a wire brush and some emery cloth. No wonder it didn't start. Once I got back with the clean plug replaced, he jiggled the choke and sprayed some more fire juice in the air cleaner. He decided against the Gregorian chant. I refused to dance around the generator or join him in his ritualistic Monk-like trance in an effort to suck up to the generator gods. That's all I needed, heck I had an inner child for that. However, soon enough, the little power plant coughed to life and ran well enough to provide heat and water to their house. I asked him why he didn't buy a newer, more reliable unit, as this one was an antique. His response, "What for? This one runs great!"

With that, I returned home, hoping there were no more calls, texts, messages, smoke signals, or that I would see the Batman sign in the sky over my little cottage. So my morning was filled with unexpected surprises. I went to the aid of three neighbors and ended up NOT helping either one, it would seem. Do you think it was just for emotional support? Maybe they just wanted to see my ripped rain pants. The pants were in the trash the same day.

After lunch, I looked outside at my very crooked portable car enclosure. The roadside front end was still sitting in the driveway and was unusable. It looked pitiful with its sagging sides, broken bungee cords and loose anchors strewn about. The heavy rain had subsided some and the winds were half of what they were mid-morning. I decided not to do anything until the next day. Besides the damaged garage, the property looked like a demolition site. What a mess. What was I to do? Hey, I had vodka and Coke. I'd sit and give it more thought. Something good always comes out of a timeout and a good stiff drink. Which I deserved! I was having a day!

As my karma got better, no thanks to you know who, two days would pass when the cavalry arrived in the form of my always helpful daughter and her very talented husband. Between 10 a.m. and 1 p.m. on Wednesday, some thirty-six hours later, we had dismantled the broken garage and started in on straightening the large curve the heavy wind had inflicted on the frame. We ended up replacing one six-foot piece of piping, and then went to work to place the whole enclosure back where it belonged. Once back in place, we then replaced all the bungee cords on the enclosure, which totaled about eighty. Next, we reset all the in-ground anchors, pounding the anchor wedges about 12 inches in the still not frozen earth. By 1 p.m. or so, we had repaired the portable garage and soon drove the GMC back in its resting place. We had saved the enclosure.

While the son-in-law and I were working on that project, my wife and daughter asked me what they could do to help. I mentioned that they could walk the property and remove the large tree branches and put them in a pile for me to pick up later. To my surprise, they went to work and raked the entire property. They ended up picking up some 12 to 15 forty-gallon trash cans full of debris and disposed of it in a nearby empty lot. (Makes great fill.) They worked very hard and brought much joy to the day. I was very thankful for both of them.

It was a great day, and I was very content with everything that got done. I guess helping others during the storm paid off. God sent two angels to get me through my unfortunate dilemma. Why? Because He knew my inner child wouldn't help. See, God has a sense of humor!

Now I need to go shopping for a new pair of rain pants. Where's my Amazon gift card?

ramp-age

It was a cool, cloudy and dreary morning on the lake, enduring a spring season that had boasted more rain than sun. Yet there was a tropical warmth in the air that settled along the shores of the lake. With a welcomed break in shower activity in the area, I strolled onto the front deck overlooking my kingdom when I heard the familiar sound of a truck backing a boat down the private right of way into the shallow waters of the busy ramp. It was a 16-foot well-maintained bow rider with white vinyl interior and an off-white fiberglass hull. Two men got out of the truck and went about the ritual of loosening all the straps and tie-downs that kept the boat secured to the four-wheeled trailer.

Once the boat was free of its bindings, the truck backed the boat into the shallow water, but not enough to float it off easily. Why do people think that just because they're in the water, the boat will magically start floating? I've written several tales of misadventures in boat handling, but this is one of the best yet. These guys get an "A" for Absurd.

It all began with the two men trying to bull the boat off the trailer from the front end. Each man took a side at the bow and began pushing the heavy trailered boat off the back of the trailer, all to no avail. Try as they might, the boat would not move. I was going to yell out, "Move the truck back five feet, and it floats off." But what would be the fun in that? Now moving to the sides of the boat, they tried rocking it sideways to loosen the boat from the carpeted bunk rails. That didn't work either. Why? Still not enough water under the boat. Now getting tired, they took a break to come up with another plan. I was enjoying this one!

After a short breather, one of the men climbed into the boat and started the 60 hp Mercury motor. Still in shallow water, he tried powering the boat in reverse, hoping to move the boat. The propeller of the motor was barely in the water, providing no traction or grip that would be beneficial. He produced a thick, oily, smelly dark cloud that only serve to kill some mosquitoes, a grouping of wild flowers, and turn the ramp water a dark muddy color. Good job, men! I don't feel so itchy!

Then it went from rampage to rambunctious. The man in the boat thought that if he ran from the front of the boat to the rear and rammed his shoulder in the rear cushion, he could dislodge the boat from the trailer bunks, and push the boat backwards, thus sliding it off the trailer. The only thing I could see getting dislodged would be his shoulder. Not once, but twice and again thrice (I mean three times) he ran full speed from the front of the boat to the rear, plowing his shoulder into the rear cushion, reminiscent of a football player pushing those steel sleds in practice. Of course, that didn't work either. What was he thinking? He had to have a very sore shoulder. Then, a lightbulb went on over his head. I could see it from my perch 100 feet away.

Are you sitting down?

The man in the water said (You can't make up this stuff.), "If you rush down the center again and ram the back cushion while I try pushing the front end, maybe both of us can get it off."

I wondered just how long this absurdity was going to last. I knew my vodka stock was good, but was it this good? So without giving it a second thought, and, working together, the running fullback and the front end pusher worked together in tandem and got absolutely nowhere. Yep, that was expected. The boat sat on the trailer exactly where it had been from the time they arrived. Yet, I was having a really nice time.

After another short rest, they came up with another bright idea. Now both were out of the water, standing near the trailer tongue. They stretched out horizontally between the front of the boat and the truck's tailgate, trying hard to push the boat off the trailer with brute force. Are you kidding me? I was listening for bones to break. That didn't work either, and yet, I still wasn't compelled to go help them. The answer was so easy.

Finally, after several more agonizing minutes of tomfoolery, they finally came up with a solution that might easily work. Wait for it!

The driver thought that maybe if he backed up the truck a few feet, that the boat might slide off the trailer. And in doing just that, the boat easily lifted off the trailer and floated on the calm waters of the ramp. The day was saved. The shoulder... not so much!

Maybe I should give a course in proper boat launching here at the ramp. I wonder if Shoulder Guy needs a drink.

the ride

I was enjoying a warm Saturday morning on the lake, taking in the brilliant sun, the light breeze, and the smell of burning gas and oil wafting over my property from all the boats coming onto the nearby boat ramp on Corbin Way. Yeah, it was the beginning of summer, and all the sights, sounds and smells that came with it made Bauneg Beg Lake a special place. I had completed my weekly grounds maintenance work and had put everything away so I could enjoy the rest of the weekend. I had plenty of Coke and vodka to help me pass the time and had started another novel by one of my favorite authors.

Resting on the deck, overlooking the vast expanse of calm water reaching toward the peninsula, I was taken in by the bright sunshine, the calm breeze, the smell of the warming pines, and the cawing sounds of the turkey vultures eclipsing the sun. Wait!! Turkey vultures! The lake had ducks, loons, eagles, pigeons, crows, and an assortment of other flying little crap factories I didn't know the names of, but I'd never seen turkey vultures fly so close to the cottage. I checked my beverage, but it was the same strength I'd become fond of, so that wasn't it. Maybe I was being a little paranoid, but I could swear the five large birds were eyeing me as their next meal. They landed in a nearby tree, straining the large limb as they grouped together, searching for their next meal. I didn't move from my chair, as they were only two trees away. Did I mention they were big birds? However, after fifteen minutes, and with no visible indication that any lunch would be had soon, they lifted off and headed north toward the local golf course. Yeah, go get those golf balls!

As the day progressed, the ramp maintained its busy schedule of boats and jet skis being launched, providing me with more antics and shenanigans from self-proclaimed would-be sailors. It was a great day for sure. And there was no sign of those pesky turkey vultures.

About mid-afternoon, I was reminded by my better half that it was time for me to get ready for church, after which we would join our friends for supper at a nearby eatery. So, after some much needed grooming and a change of clothes much befitting my presence in The Lord's House, I was ready for the rest of my day.

Walking back out onto the deck, I saw a neighbor pulling up to my dock in his yellow and white, two seat, Sea-Doo speed boat. I wasn't that familiar with the neighbor, yet here he was, stopping by to make his acquaintance. The boat was tossing from side to side as he stopped the engine on my approach down the dock to greet him. After some light *guy* chitchat, he asked me if I'd like to take a ride in his boat. I had my own high-powered crotch rocket nearby, but I had never ridden in a speed boat like this one.

I accepted his invitation but told him I only had fifteen minutes as I was leaving for church soon. He said we'd be back in plenty of time. I carefully stepped into the boat, took the co-pilots seat, and we were off. We were cruising at a pretty good speed, and the wind was pushing my hair straight to the back of my head. We were moving right along at eye-watering speeds. Good thing I had my glasses on, yet I found myself squinting, anyway. We were halfway down the center of the lake when my new friend decided to bank a right-hand turn at high speed. When I say a right-hand turn, I don't mean he eased the wheel over and made a wide, high-speed sweeping turn. I mean, he turned the boat at 90 degrees instantly. I think his intent was to put the boat in a high-speed short radius turn, causing a large rooster tail of white water to reach high in the sky as we skidded sideways like we were in a boat show in Florida.

My 240-pound frame became weightless and instantly jerked me out of my seat, flying into his lap. I was grabbing at anything so I would not be thrown into the water. I ended up straddling him in a very unmanly way, trying to keep my glasses on my face and not wetting myself as the boat finally slowed down. I was able to get back in my seat, making a manly comment like, "Man, this boat is really fast!"

Not sure how many people witnessed this near catastrophe, and I didn't really care. I needed the ride (however well-intended it was) to be over so I could get myself rearranged to get to church. Seems I had a lot to thank God for. Once the boat settled down, the neighbor then informed me that my seat had a seat belt. Yeah, he never mentioned that and had assumed I had put it on. Not!

We finally arrived back at my dock with minutes to spare before heading off to church. I looked like I'd been through a nasty fight with those turkey vultures. In no time, I was presentable again. I was thankful no one got hurt, and that despite the unusual introduction, I had made a new friend. Hey, he gave me a ride in his boat! He did apologize and we still laugh about it years later.

Not sure which was worse, the high-speed boat ride or the possibility of being lunch for the turkey vultures. Either way, it was another memorable day on the lake.

God, I love this place!

flames

I t all started in early February 2019, or it could have been 2020. The summer season leading to the winter months of that particular year provided me with days upon days of ample work around the cottage on the shores of our beautiful southern Maine lake. There was always some task that needed to be taken care of. Although the work varied, there was always one weekly task that had to get done. I had to cut the grass, do some light trimming, air clean the walkways and driveway, rake the beach area and keep the place looking as pristine as I could. Hey, you never know when company will show up.

Some days, after relatively stiff daylong winds, I'd find my property littered with larger than normal tree branches and other assorted debris. Once gathered, I would usually pile all that stuff in the back of my truck and haul it off to the local landfill, where I was charged $5 per cubic yard for the disposal. Living under dozens of 90-foot pine, maple, and oak trees, it wasn't unusual that I would do a dump run two or three times a year to discard the unwanted tree debris that fell from on high. (Almost sounds biblical, doesn't it?)

One day, while I was stacking unwanted tree debris in my truck, my friendly next-door neighbor walked over to make light chit chat as he was accustomed to doing whenever we were both outside. Over the summer, he had started a "burn pile" on the edge of his property, within 15 feet or so of the water's edge. He had much more property and many more trees than I did, and he had piled all his debris into a now growing burn pile.

Neighbor: "Instead of going to the dump, you can put all the branches and stuff on the burn pile if you want. Save you a trip and some money too. I'll burn it all someday. Up in Cornish (where he actually lives), the neighbors and I take turns each year building a burn pile from tree waste, old wooden stuff and anything that will burn. One year it's my place, the next year it's the neighbor across the way, or the one up the road. Feel free to use that pile over there."

Me: "Okay, if you don't mind, I'll do just that. Let me know if you need help with it. I'm always here."

So, I drove my already loaded truck down the right of way and backed up to the small debris pile that he had started. By the time I unloaded my truck, the pile was twice the size. Since I had saved a thirty-minute trip to the dump, and at least $10, I had time for a refreshing beverage. Yeah, this was a little piece of heaven all right.

As I said earlier, it was evening in mid-February when the bright lights first caught my eye. The lovely wife and I had settled down to watch another Hallmark tear-jerker movie. (Me, I played a casino game on my iPhone.) Not really paying attention to the movie, I soon fell asleep in my La-Z-Boy, not a care in the world.

Suddenly, the wife started yelling, "What the heck is that?" Her sudden excited remark woke me with a start. As I opened my eyes and got them into focus, the entire cottage was lit up like Miami Beach. It was so bright in the cottage, I wondered if I was in a Twilight Zone episode. (Remember that show?)

As soon as I shot out of my recliner (I didn't know a large man could move that fast), the side window facing the neighbor's property caught my attention. And... there it was. A huge fire was underway. From what I could see, the burning pile looked as wide as 30 feet across at the base and more than 20 feet high, with large yellow flames reaching for the sky. The brightness lit up all the cottages within 200 feet. The flames could be seen from across the lake, through the tree lined peninsula and onto the shores of North Berwick. I couldn't believe how big the fire was. I was a little concerned for my home, of course.

Looking more closely out the window, I could see the singular shadow of my neighbor leaning on a rake, without a care in the world. I could see the flames getting higher and lapping the bark of the nearby pine trees. I could see small flickers and sparks coming off the tree's sides, facing the roaring fire. I had a choice: vodka and Coke and enjoy the show, or get dressed and go out there to help fight the fire. I chose the latter, of course, although the neighbor didn't seem as excited as I was.

While I was getting dressed, my cellphone alerted me to an incoming call. It was my friend Tarzan up the cove asking me if my house was on fire. From his vantage point, my little cottage appeared totally engulfed. Before heading out, I had another call asking if we were safe. I told them both we were fine and that my neighbor was doing housecleaning. Seemed to be the right thing to say at the time.

I finally got outside and quickly approached the neighbor, and was greeted with a calm, "Hey, how you doing?" I mentioned this unexpected surprise and the calls I was getting about my safety. After some talk, he mentioned that he had gotten a fire permit and had a water hose handy in case he needed it. I asked, "You think them 25-foot high flames and scorching bark might need some water?" He replied, "Not really, there's plenty of snow on the ground and I want to kill that tree, anyway. It may take a few fires, though!" The neighbor sure had a cavalier attitude about this blaze.

After being out there for fifteen minutes, I saw the red flashing lights of a town fire truck come to a stop in the front of his house. The two fire fighters walked down to where we were standing. Neither seemed concerned.

Neighbor: "Hi, how are you?"

Fire Guys: "Doing great. I see you have a nice warm fire going tonight. It's cold enough for one."

Neighbor: "Yeah, I thought I'd clean up my burn pile before it got too big." (Really neighbor, too big??) He continued, "Here's a copy of my permit," and handed it to them.

Fire Guys: "Well, the permit is in good order, and you have a garden hose nearby, and you have a tender with you, so you're all set. Be careful and have a good night." Just like that, they were off.

Neighbor: "Good night."

So, I was a tender, huh? Good thing I went out to join him. We got along well and he was a good neighbor. The fire went out after three hours, and the pile was reduced to nothing more than a small pile of smoldering ashes with a 30-foot radius. The tree bark was still smoking some.

Since that first sphincter-churning bonfire, the neighbor comes to my back door each year, arms filled with dry kindling and matches, letting me know he's about to start a blaze. I then immediately go on a social media page to alert folks around the lake that a bonfire will take place. It stops the phone calls, anyway.

Funny thing... every year, the friendly fire fighters show up to the bonfire to make sure we're safe. I wonder who keeps calling them?

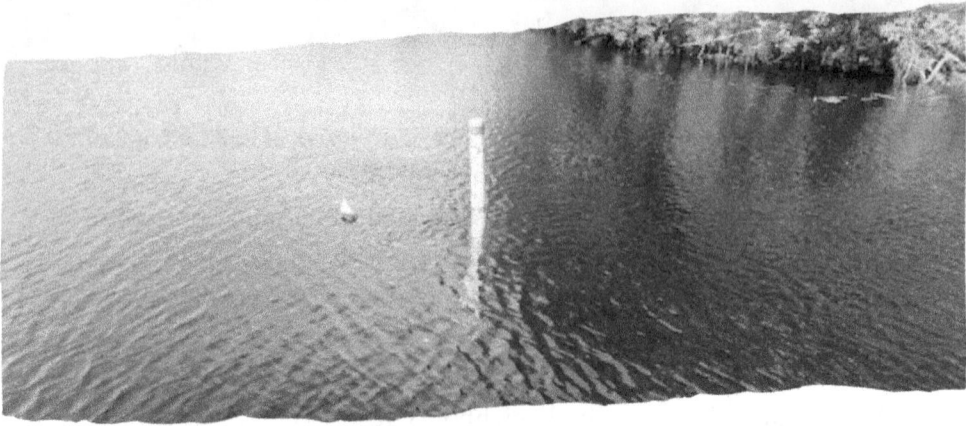

nearly banished

I t was another warm and sunny day on beautiful Bauneg Beg
Lake. The water was calm in Patriot Cove. While there was a
slight breeze, the calmness was mostly because there was little
to no boating activity to stir up the water. And being the middle of the
week, there was much less hubbub going on to upset the serenity I
was enjoying. The weekends were a whole different matter, of course.
I was sitting on my awning covered deck enjoying a cold beverage
and reading a novel by my favorite author when my ever present cellphone pinged, alerting me to an incoming call. I didn't recognize the
number and thought better of answering it, thinking it was another
bothersome robo-call.

It was my sister. She lived in North Carolina these days with her
husband and two large dogs. While she had come to Maine recently
to visit our family for a week, her husband stayed home to work, care
for the puppies, and do whatever needed to be done at home while
she was away. We had invited her and Mom (whom she was staying
with) for lunch and she was letting me know that she was bringing
her son and grandson with her. I was glad to have them all come to
the lake for lunch and a visit. Family time was always welcomed. Her
son and his son lived in Rhode Island these days. Maine was as close

as they got to each other, where a *visit* would be good for all of them. Seems like today was the day to gather at the cottage and get reacquainted, as it were.

As they arrived, the required hugs and kisses went around the kitchen before everyone settled down on the deck, taking up light chit chat. Typical stuff about the job, school, and anything else that came up was shared. Thankfully, lunch was finally served by the better half. We enjoyed some grilled chicken, potato salad, and pie for dessert. Not sure why, but I did have a tumbler with vodka and Coke on ice. Yep, it was a good day for it. Always is.

The nephew noticed that I had a pontoon boat and a Sea-Doo Bombardier Supercharge jet ski moored to the waterfront dock. He must have thought his uncle was rich. He didn't seem at all interested in the 20-foot Tahoe pontoon boat, but the Sea-Doo brought a gleam to his eyes. Not wanting to seem inhospitable, I asked:

Me: "Have you ever ridden a jet ski?"

Nephew: "Oh yeah, I've ridden them a few times. I have a friend in Rhode Island who let me use his a couple of times. They're fun."

Me: "Okay, but did you ever drive one by yourself or were you just a passenger?"

Nephew: "I drove them a few times, no problem."

Me: "Would you like to take this one out for a ride around the lake? The lake isn't too big and today is a good day for it. It's good weather and very few other boats out there."

Nephew: Without hesitation. "Yeah, that would be cool."

I could see the excitement in his eyes at what was coming. I just hoped I wasn't making a big mistake. Why did I have this nagging feeling? Why was my inner child quiet for once? He was my 20-something nephew, but I really didn't know him. Because we didn't live close to each other, or rarely spoke, we were more like estranged relatives than any typical uncle and nephew. But I digress. He was my nephew, and I wanted him to enjoy the lake and its amenities like I would any other family member. I downed my beverage. Something felt odd inside. Ever get those feelings?

77

Before I even left the deck, I had things I wanted him to know before he set out cruising the shores of the lake.

Me: "Look, there are things you really need to pay attention to while you're out there on this machine. One: It's high powered, so remember that you have your son on the back with you. You could throw him off the back, making high-speed turns. There are also things that are important that you need to be mindful of:

- Stay away from shore by at least 50 feet; no closer unless you're coming back here.
- Don't go near any of the birds, especially near the loons. Go way around them, look for them ahead of time so you don't make last minute hard turns.
- Stay away from canoes, kayaks, and paddle boarders and sailboats if you see any out there.
- If you see the float plane, stay to the side of the lake and give it a wide berth until he takes off or comes in for a landing.
- If you go into any coves, slow down and just cruise in and out. Don't leave a wake. You'll see the no wake buoys.

"Any questions?"

Nephew: "No, I got it."

However, the "let's go" look on his face made me feel like I was making a mistake. But here we were. What could possibly go wrong? It was then that my inner child started to giggle.

The machine was full of fuel (13 gallons), and he and his son had donned the latest in Coast Guard approved Type III personal flotation devices, cinched appropriately, and were ready to ride. I turned the machine toward the center of the cove and let them mount up. I gave the nephew a short tutorial on the start, stop, and when to lean into turns. He kept saying he was good. He just wanted to hit the throttle and get out on the water. As the instructions were ending, he hit the gas and the jet pump on the high-powered machine sent a rooster tail of water my way, getting me soaking wet. Okay, I thought, we're off to a great start.

I returned to the deck and joined the ladies, wondering how long the ride would last. He left the cove, taking a hard left toward the main body of the lake. At one point, we saw the machine skimming the water as they cruised up the east side of the peninsula. I thought he was pretty close to land, but... as they made their way to the north end of the lake, they made a sweeping turn and raced down the center of the cove at high speed. Looks like they were having a great time, and I was worrying for nothing. I calmed myself with an all too familiar beverage. Life was good.

About forty-five minutes later (I don't put forty-five minutes on the machine all summer), the nephew came back to the dock. I went down to the beach to meet him and tell him when to shut off the engine. I didn't need another damaged wear ring to work on. He slowed up as he approached, shut off the engine, and had a huge grin on his face. The force of the wind made their long hair stand straight back like they were standing in front of a high-powered fan. They had a really good ride and thanked me for it. Made their day. I was glad they were back, and the machine was safely back on the dock.

The boys returned to the upper deck, telling us what a great time they'd had. We gathered around the patio table and had a dessert of chocolate cream pie Mom had brought for us. Mom always brought dessert when she came to the lake. (I invited her often!) While sitting there, thinking my beverage isn't that great with the pie, my phone went off, alerting me to some earth-shattering news I had to know about. Looking at the Facebook message almost took my breath away.

There, for all to see, was MY jet ski pounding the waves at very high speeds going into Otter Cove, sending a rooster tail of white water 20 feet to the sides, and nearly running over two mating Loons in the process. The entirety of Otter Cove was a No Wake Zone with a State of Maine Buoy prominently anchored in the CENTER of the cove's narrow entrance. A blind man could see it. You actually had to go around it to avoid hitting it. Yet, here was the unmistakable image of the nephew and his son whipping through the normally quiet cove, bouncing docked boats, causing potential erosion problems, affecting the wildlife, not knowing a concerned and angry resident was filming the whole thing. Yeah, I needed a really stiff drink. And why was my inner child roaring with glee? What the heck is wrong with her?

I didn't want to embarrass my sister or her two offspring, so I kept as quiet as I could without wanting to scream my lungs out. About mid-afternoon, they said their goodbyes and left for home. Once gone, I showed the wife the dramatic footage on my Facebook page. Everybody on the lake saw the footage. The author made some comment about some idiots who came into his realm at high-speed nearly killing our prized loons in the process. I couldn't deny his observations or that it wasn't my machine being used as a weapon. A couple of folks had chimed in calling for police intervention, organizing a lake posse, or going dock-to-dock to find the perp. I was embarrassed, to say the least, and here I was a Board Member and Fundraising Chair for the lake Association. The shame! What could I do!

There was no doubt! I immediately went into the comments under the video and claimed full responsibility for the actions. I apologized in earnest for this lake faux pas, explaining that it was my machine and a family member who was visiting from out of town. I promised it would never happen again and the culprit would never again ride my jet ski on the lake. That was easy to do since he was going back to Rhode Island two days later. I hoped he didn't want to stop in for another ride before he left.

After a few more folks (they can't help themselves) commented about knowing better, making me grovel like the penitent I was, the lake family finally said they understood and forgave me. The video was removed that night. I'm sure such infractions happened before and they will happen again. But not to me. Nobody called for my banishment from the lake or the board I served on.

The following spring I sold the high-powered crotch rocket to a lake neighbor. I wasn't using it much, anyway. I don't miss it, never have.

It's so much better to sit on the deck, enjoy a cold beverage on a warm day (it doesn't have to be warm really), and fall asleep reading a novel by my favorite author.

I love the people who live here. They're so forgiving!

the reunion

It was an unusually warm morning on the lake. Although it was early February, the warm temperatures in the high 40s and the warm sun seemed uncharacteristic for this time of year in Maine. It had been unusual in that so far; we had not weathered any Nor' easters or any other major storm event. Of course, winter was far from over.

It was four days before the anticipated Super Bowl when my phone trilled, alerting me to an incoming call. It was the lake association Vice President, Limoncello Bob. Creator and producer of the lake borne, ever popular, highly sought golden nectar of the gods, 80 day fermented and twice filtered Limoncello. After our usual light, friendly banter, he got to the point.

Bob: "Hey, are you busy on Sunday, and would you like to come to the house to watch the Super Bowl?"

Me: "That would be great. Thanks so much for the invitation. We'll bring dessert if that's okay."

Bob: "You don't have to bring anything but whatever you want to drink, but dessert would be good. I'm gathering the rest of 'The Cave' members for this game. I'm really glad you can come."

Listing off the four couples that would be in attendance, I was happy to be invited. I had hoped to stay home this year and enjoy the game, even deferring an invitation to my son's home to enjoy the big game. We went there almost every year, but this year, for whatever reason, I had declined his generous offer to stay home. Until the call came. The invitation had a purpose.

For more than twenty years, selected close friends gathered in The Cave every Sunday from September to February to watch the favored New England Patriots. The small Patriot Museum was located in the basement area of The Mayor's home on the shores of beautiful Bauneg Beg Lake, and each week, the room was filled with good friends, great food, too much laughter, and the best memories of good times shared. It all came to an end in December 2019, when our beloved mayor passed away. It was he who gathered the football faithful each week into the inner sanctum he called The Cave. He made room for everyone, and everyone was welcomed.

Those gathered each week included: The Mayor, Limoncello Bob, Patti Girl, The Black Russian, The Sound Effects, The Architect, Salty, The Plumber, The Lake Princess, Two Lakes Over, and me, The Deputy. Sometimes we had guests join us like Tarzan and Lady Gaga. They received these monikers from me over the many years of writing lake stories. It made each story more interesting and enjoyable. Well, for me anyway.

After The Mayor passed away, it was Mrs. Mayor who offered us all the use of The Cave for the 2020 Super Bowl. While it was a great gesture, not one person felt comfortable, nor did anyone even have the desire to return to The Cave that year. It was too soon after The Mayor's passing and we all stayed home. Funny thing about human nature.

Since The Mayor's passing, other Cave members have passed on as well. Salty, The Plumber, and The Architect. The remaining Cave members stayed in touch through the years and were all neighbors on the lake, but had never gotten together for a football game since. Not even a Super Bowl. Regardless of the teams involved.

Now, five years later, we were being summoned for a Super Bowl reunion at the home of Limoncello Bob and Patti Girl. And the remaining Cave members all agreed to come. There would be four couples in all. Besides our genial hosts, the gathering would include The Lake Princess, Two Lakes Over, The Black Russian, Mr. Sound Effects, me, The Deputy, and my lovely First Mate. Star of the night was Gnig, the dog. (Pronounced: ga-nook.)

The big game between the Kansas City Chiefs and the favored San Francisco 49ers was scheduled for a 6:39.0568 kick-off. By 4:45 in the afternoon, the invitees had all arrived, happy to see each other. After rounds of hugs and handshakes, we gathered around the large dining room table (set for eight) and feasted on seasoned fried shrimp that Bob had sautéed for us. Once we all sat down, he retrieved an ice cold bottle of Limoncello from the kitchen freezer and rejoined us with eight tall shot glasses. We knew what was coming. Bob's shot glasses are not like the regular 1 oz. glasses. Bob's idea of a shot glass is something in the range of a small brandy snifter. Go big or go home! After a few shots, you're lucky if you make it home. Let the good times roll.

It was our gracious host who began the rounds of long-awaited toasts. And what better to toast with than the ever popular Limoncello? So, with filled shot glasses lifted high, it began:

Bob: "Here's to Roger. I know he's looking down and celebrating with us. Ching Ching."

With a resounding "here, here" and "salute", we raised the glasses in honor of our departed friend, The Mayor, who always made Super Bowl Sunday a festival of friends, food, football, and fun.

Again....

Bob: "Here's to all the others who have passed and can't be with us tonight."

Another collective clinking of glasses in remembrance of those who passed since our last meeting in the Cave.

The Lake Princess: "And here's to all of us present, and too many more reunions ahead."

With that final toast, we had drained our shot glasses and were ready to start dinner that was prepared for us by our hosts. While we ate, we reminisced about past years in The Cave and the many characters who made those gatherings special and memorable.

Soon it was time to gather in the living room and for the start of the Super Bowl. Half the group was rooting for the 49ers, and the other half wanted the Chiefs to win. So, as usual, we were off to a fun start. If the Patriots had been in the game, it would have been a unanimous decision, but not tonight. It was in the second quarter that the 49ers took the lead with a field goal, and the cheering from the 49ers' fans in the room was deafening. We celebrated with a shot of Limoncello. As the game progressed, the lead kept changing sides and by the end of the game, the teams had tied at 19-19. Lots more Limoncello was poured with every score. For the first time in twenty-eight years, (or 128, I'm not sure) the Super Bowl went into overtime.

Several things happened right then. One, our hosts, Limoncello Bob and Patti Girl, were creatures of habit, and over the many years had gone to bed by 8 p.m. every evening. They even had a 'friendly' sign in their kitchen that read, "We're glad you're here, but please go home by 8 p.m." Not today, my friends, not today. The worse thing that could happen was entertaining a late day game and then have it go into overtime. We were looking at at least 11 p.m. now. It seems that when you want to see the end of the game, it takes forever, especially with long drawn out commercials you could care less about. Or couldn't care less about. Well, you know what I mean. Not to mention the geriatric yawning going around the room. The 49ers took more than eight minutes in overtime to finally be in position to kick a field goal and bring the score to 22-19, but the Chiefs were allowed a possession as well, so the game wasn't over just yet.

Suddenly, sitting next to The Lake Princess, she started making circular motions in front of herself, telling Bob, "I'm moving all the bad juju out of this room so the Chiefs can win." Having witnessed her *spirit guide* tactics in the past, all she got was stares. But those who knew her were a little taken aback. The woman had some serious magic, and I believed in her.

The Chiefs did get the ball back and promptly marched down the field, 75 yards to end the game with a touchdown and went on to win with a 25-22 score that brought the stadium in Vegas to an uproarious unexpected celebration, and the small gathering on Bauneg Beg Lake to a quiet end to the night.

It was near 11 p.m. when the remaining guests departed. It had been a wonderful reunion enjoyed by all. It didn't matter what the score was or who won the game. We were the winners on this Super Bowl Sunday, having kept alive the memories of the past and remained hopeful of what the future would bring.

God, I love this place.

rizzo

L et me introduce you to my furry four-legged grand dog, Rizzo! Rizzo loves coming to see his grandparents on the shores of beautiful Bauneg Beg Lake any time of year. He enjoys boating season the most, but enjoys his winter stays too, at what we call the Bauneg Beg Barf-O-Rama and Boutique. Rizzo is a three-year-old King Charles spaniel. He has a very handsome face, soft eyes, and thinks he's a lap dog at his fighting weight of twenty-three pounds. No matter where I sit, Rizzo is on my lap before my butt hits the seat.

During his visits, I try to keep him on a regular schedule for relieving himself of any DNA he needs to get rid of. He's used to the schedule we keep, knowing that if he's a "good boy", some kind of treat will be awarded for his good behavior. After a successful outing and our return to the cottage, he instantly camps out in front of the cabinet holding his treats and fidgets like a live wire until the tasty little bites are in his possession. I have to watch my fingers pretty closely when feeding him, as I've been unintentionally scarred in the past. Those little teeth can be sharp.

So, if you know me, you know that sometimes I talk to inanimate objects, or they talk to me. Well, my little friend Rizzo talks to me fairly often when we're together, especially when we're out for a DNA deposit. Might be the vodka or the Limoncello. Either way, I hear him.

Our typical outing is anything but typical. The dance begins when I don my brain bucket (hat) and my coat if needed. Rizzo bounces on his paws, anticipating his outing and the treat he knows will follow. He gets so excited, at times it's difficult to get the leash on his collar. Once he's securely hooked up for safety, we're ready to go. Well, he is. I'd rather stay back, read a good book, maybe imbibe a fresh beverage. But no, duty calls. (I said duty!) And here is how a particular walk went today that prompted this story.

We left the house and entered the enclosed entryway like we've done a hundred times. Something must have caught his eye, as he instantly turned towards the right side wall and wrapped himself around the small round wicker table, thus getting himself stuck there. I asked him, "What the heck are you doing? There's nothing there. Get over here so I can undo your leash."

Having re-leashed the puppy, he went to the door, stood on his hind legs, looking out the door window, surveying the area he has claimed as his domain. I opened the door to the outside, and he instantly ran to the left near the gambrel shed in hopes of snatching a small chipmunk or other rodent that resides beneath the large structure. As usual, and luckily, there's nothing to find.

Going down the walkway toward the road, he extended his leash to the full 16 feet and started yanking my arm to its full extension. I guess I wasn't walking fast enough. We quickly found the end of the driveway where the fun began.

Rizzo: "Which way do we go? Right? Left? Let me take a sniff and see if I notice anything. That okay Gramps? That okay?"

Me: "I don't really care. Just pick a way, and let's go."

Rizzo: "I think I smell something this way."

Like a live wire, he moved quickly to the left, and we started our trek up the street. The leash was still fully extended and my arm was out in front of me, straining to keep hold of the leash. He suddenly stopped.

Me: "You can't just bury your snout under those piles of crap. You don't know what's under there."

Rizzo: "I'll only be a minute. I smell something. Smells like old female dog leavings. Interesting scent."

Me: "Okay, you've been buried in there long enough, and it's cold out here, so let's go."

I gave his leash a small yank, and he refused to budge, sticking solidly to his newfound plot. The gentle nudge turned into a pulling contest that I won, but only because of our weight differential. Moving a little further up the street, we stopped again at another scent he'd discovered.

NOTE: This street has more than a dozen dogs that live here. So it stands to reason that over a period of time, there will be an overabundance of deposits up and down the street, some unseen and unfortunately some out in the open. (Shameful). Either way, Rizzo found each and every one along his path. Moving up the street, he stopped abruptly at another interesting spot.

Rizzo: "Hey, this one smells fresh. Come down here and smell this one."

Me: "I don't think so. Just hurry up."

Rizzo: "Come on, take a sniff."

Me: "I said no."

Rizzo: "TAKE A SNIFF!!!"

Yelling at me. Really dog?

Once he was done surveying this pile of whatever was so interesting, we moved on until he finally decided he should leave his own deposit for some other dog pal to find and enjoy. However, being a responsible dog walker, I stooped down to pick up his DNA leavings, and we moved on.

Me: "Okay, this is far enough. Let's cross the street."

Rizzo: "Good, because I smell something over there under that fence. Let's go there, Grumps."

Me: "It's Gramps, not Grumps."

Rizzo: "Should have thought of that earlier when I offered to share that fine scent with you, Fat Boy!"

Me: "Are you kidding me?"

Rizzo: "Let's get over there. I smell some good stuff."

So, we crossed the street and sure enough, Rizzo crawled under the split-rail fence and discovered a new whatever he discovered. Could be anything, but he had his nose buried to his eyeballs. Must be a good find. He better not ask me to sniff it again. After a short time, he straightened out and started to sneeze. After two short outbursts through his small nose, he shook his head, and we moved on.

Rizzo: "Yeah, you don't want to smell that one. That's bad juju right there. You're welcome."

We moved down the street and headed for home. Finally, although it had only been ten minutes, it seemed like forever. Then he stopped to relieve himself again, knowing it would be some time before he got this chance again. And he did have a treat waiting.

Me: "Let's go home and see Grammy. It's cold out here and I've had enough."

Rizzo: "It's not that cold, Sissy Boy."

Me: "You're six feet lower at ground level. I'm up here in the wind. There's no wind down there. Yeah, it's cold."

Rizzo: "Grrrr!"

We finally returned to the familiar driveway, and he took an indirect path to the back door. He continued sniffing the ground like a bloodhound on a mission until he stopped at the entryway door, waiting for me to let him in. Once inside, he again went left and wrapped himself around the table.

Me: "What the heck are you doing, Rizzo?"

Rizzo: "I thought I saw a bug."

After de-leashing him, we finally entered the warmth of the cottage, where he quickly sat in front of the cabinet holding his treats. Once he received his two small Milk Bone treats, he settled down to rest. As soon as I sat on the couch, he was on me before my butt hit the cushion. I guess we're closer than I thought. In a couple of short hours, we get to do this dance all over again. Yeah, I need a beverage!

And the stay at Bauneg Beg Lake Barf-O-Rama and Boutique continues for another seven days and many more fun outings with my furry friend. I'll need more DNA bags! And a refreshing beverage.

being first

For over the two and a half decades I've lived on this beautiful lake, I've always found that the spring season was the most competitive and anticipated time of year for folks who live here. Each year, residents are anxious to get their docks installed to await the boats, jet skis, canoes, paddle boards, rafts, and whatever that will grace their waterfronts all summer long. Of course, timing is everything, and everything hinges on Mother Nature having a good attitude. The Mayor and I always looked toward dock in day as a springtime ritual, always trying to be the first docks in on the lake. While it was not a contest, it did give us bragging rights around the lake, though I doubt anyone cared. But we did, and we celebrated with a cold brew after achieving the tasks.

Most years, The Mayor and I docked in together, but my respect for his title, and his need for achievement, allowed us to put his dock in first, then we would put my docks in. (A good deputy mayor knows his place.) While the installations were all done within a couple of hours and a beer or two, we were usually the first docks in. Then, until the boats were delivered from the marina, all we had to do was sit on his manicured lawn, enjoy the sun, have a beer, and wonder how the other half lived. Life was good on the shores of beautiful Bauneg Beg Lake.

Of course, there were other folks who tried to get the jump on dock in, with the intent of tipping The Mayor out of first place and claim bragging rights for that particular year. I remember one year when our friend Salty installed his 24 feet of aluminum dock located at the north end of the lake. The lake had not yet shed its icy mantle, although the north end where Salty lived was clear of ice. Having little to do one nice early spring day, he proceeded to install his 24 feet of metal docking, claiming his first-place deed.

It was two days later that a mid-spring weather storm rolled through the lake. Along with some minor snow came strong winds. The weather pattern lasted for a full day. While the snow melted quickly, strong winds prevailed through the night. The next morning, Salty saw that his aluminum dock was bent upward, reaching toward the sky. The dock had been forcibly bent at the connecting joint to the second section of dock. The outward piece jutted 12 feet straight up in the air and looked like Mother Nature was giving him the middle finger. A large middle finger at that. During that night, the 40-knot winds blew northerly, driving a large mass of thick ice directly into his recently installed docking system. Being first sometimes has its issues, it seems. Maybe it's not a good idea to mess with The Mayor. Or Mother Nature.

Luckily, it was another lake neighbor that came to the rescue. Our resident pilot, Two Lakes Over, was consulted on this tragic metal bending issue. Having extreme expertise in the mechanical trades, he took on the project of making repairs to the bent docking and returned it to its pristine condition to be used safely for another summer. If you want to be first, you really need to have friends.

On a recent day, the last day of winter 2024, we had another incident that was interesting. We had witnessed an unusually warm February that extended for more than two weeks into March without any snow or major storms, and had warm temperatures in the 50s for several days. During that time, the entire snowpack had melted, and due to strong winds, the lakebed had watered out by March 7th. That was unheard of for Maine. The lake had iced out at least five weeks ahead of time. That was a lake record.

As human nature would dictate, an overanxious lake neighbor decided to put his docks in earlier than usual and call for his boat in what seemed the ideal time of the month. Warm day, calm water, sunny skies. Yeah, I had thoughts of the upcoming dock in but knew from past experience Mother Nature was not done with winter just yet. However, the lake neighbor forged ahead into spring.

The following morning, I saw a red pickup truck drive down our lane towing a 16-foot pontoon boat. I knew it was not a delivery from our own Parker's Boathouse. I started to walk toward the truck, only to find the operator was from another marina. I wondered what he was doing here with the lake water level so low. I mean... really low... like 45.63940 feet out from shore low. I knew this would be a story in the making. It was too early for a cold beverage, too! I guess the neighbor never told the marina we had no water at the boat launch. Being first has its own issues sometimes.

The red pickup backed down Corbin Way and came to a stop some 20 feet from the ramp. The driver got out of the truck and removed all the tie-down straps and prepped the boat for the water. It took some ten minutes before the lake neighbor arrived on site, and after some light chit chat with the driver, he got on the boat and was ready to be launched.

The driver started backing into the ramp and continued until he hit water about 40 feet out. They had a high riding trailer, so there was a need for lots of water under the boat to make it float. The truck was as far out on the ramp as I had ever seen. As he kept backing out, the trailer was nowhere near being submerged. So he kept backing up until half of the truck was underwater. I could not see the rocker panels, so water had to be getting into the truck unless he had really good seals around the doors. Water bubbled at the rear of the truck from the exhaust system. I could see the driver was getting nervous. The boat operator then turned on the outboard motor and put it in reverse, trying hard to back off the sticky trailer.

The truck driver, seeing it wasn't working, pulled ahead a few feet, only to back up and try to jerk the boat off the trailer with a sudden stop. It didn't really work that well, considering half the truck was underwater. He was persistent, though. He did that maneuver two more times before the boat finally popped free from its cradle and floated easily on the calm lake bed. While the boat was half way across the cove toward its berth, the truck was still trying to get out of the water, all the while spilling its watery contents back onto the ramp. I wonder if there'll be an extra charge for this delivery?

You'd think this story would end here.... But no, the fun was just beginning.

The following day, the weather took a turn for the worst. The weather prognosticators, with their Doppler 4000 system that had the accuracy of Punxsutawney Phil deciding if spring would be forthcoming or nonexistent this year, had predicted the merger of two large fronts that would ride up the eastern seaboard and crash into Maine with a vengeance. That afternoon, while the storm was forming, I saw the lake neighbor riding his pontoon out on the lake looking for his diving raft that broke free of its mooring due to heavy winds. He was dressed like the Michelin man on a mission. Not sure if he found it or not. I imagine he did, although I didn't see his return trip. I was busy watching reruns of *Wagon Train* and *Gunsmoke*. (I have a schedule....)

Two days later, the storm came in with a heavy punch. We had several inches of wet, heavy snow, and on top of that, sleet and freezing rain coated everything it touched. Trees fell, power lines toppled over, and we lost electricity and internet service throughout the town. It was the worst storm in years. All the while, the pontoon sat by its dock, covered in snow and ice, and some tree debris the wind had seen fit to decorate it with, all the while braving the heavy winds, looking like a monument to winter.

I wonder if being first is really worth the effort. Me, I now have time for a cold beverage and plan my own dock in date... sometime in May! Good luck, lake neighbor. You have bragging rights for this year. You did it... you're Number One!

eclipse on bauneg beg lake

first heard about the upcoming solar eclipse in the middle of March. According to all national news agencies, on April 8th, we would witness a weather phenomenon unlike any other. A total solar eclipse was making headline news all over the country, and the news agencies were bringing this "once in a lifetime event" to fever pitch. This event would get more attention than climate change, the rat population in New York City, the price of ice in Alaska, and the Jamaican National Javelin team at the Summer Olympics. Yeah, this was a two-bottle vodka event for sure. Of course, I was ready. Like everyone else, especially on the shores of beautiful Bauneg Beg Lake, I was immediately sucked into the large circle of easily influenced people, taking this unheard-of solar system alignment as gospel.

Just to make a point before going on. This past winter was one of the mildest and driest winters on record. The lake had watered out on March 7th, weeks ahead of past years. People were already clamoring to put docks in and get the marinas to deliver their boats. It was early, but the warm days and warmer temperatures were all the inducement folks needed to act stupid... I mean impulsively. Since the onset news of this major solar event affecting millions, Mother

Nature, with her bad attitude, decided that since we were now in spring, let's have huge Nor'easters with rain, snow, ice, and powerful winds that will decimate the lands. And let's do not one, but two large storms in two weeks. Yeah, Mother Nature sure has a sense of humor. Obviously, she was not in the mood to be overshadowed, as it were, by some dim-lighted orb in the sky.

Living on the lake, under several 90 to 100-foot pine trees, is always unsettling in harsh winds. I can't even drink enough for me not to care. During the first storm, the trees shed three truckloads of branches and brush. The winds howled and the trees bent, broke, and threw us into a power loss for three days. We lost internet service, and road travel was dangerous. I had vodka, and some Depends. So... there was that.

Once the storm passed, it took me and the lovely better half two full days to clean the property and haul everything to the dump. I was tired and glad when it was over. I was hearing about the solar eclipse more and more, and started thinking, maybe there was more to this hype than I was letting myself believe. (I can be easily persuaded at times! Have you met my inner child? No? Talk about a bad storm. But I digress!)

While continuing to hear the barrage of news about the upcoming, once-in-a-lifetime, can't-be-missed, solar phenomenon, the second storm rolled in a week later on the heels of the first storm, and we, here on Bauneg Beg Lake, were the bullseye recipients of storm number two. With more howling winds, we endured some 15 inches of wet, heavy snow, accompanied by times of rain and sleet that caused more than 380,000 state-wide power outages, thousands of broken trees and telephone poles, loss of internet service and, in my case, even loss of cell service. Who goes without communication nowadays? While I have a very good Native American friend on the lake (Lake Princess), I was never taught her smoke signal techniques. Maybe this was a warning! After the four-day storm passed, we eventually got all our utilities back, but the property was in a sad state of clean up... AGAIN.

Despite the storms that had passed, the news agencies touted the upcoming April 8th solar event, with a new term I had gotten tired of hearing: the path of totality. It seems the eclipse would trek across the United States from Houston, Texas, northeast through thirteen states, ending near Houlton, Maine, before entering Canada. It was days away, and folks were coming into Maine at summer vacation levels. All the hotels, motels, and inns up north were booked by folks coming in from around the country and the world to witness this solar event of a lifetime. Everything on television was about the Eclipse. I heard, "the path of totality," many time per broadcast. Must have been the new buzz word. Remember all the buzz words we heard during the pandemic? Covid-19, social distancing, corona, masks, zoom, canceled, and Fauci. Remember those? Now we had path of totality, solar glasses, darkness, temperature drop, traffic, and other keywords. What a society we live in, huh? Thank God for good booze and a sense of humor.

The previous eclipse was in 1979, but what made this solar event different was the path it took through the center of Maine, from southwest to the northeast. It was a 150-mile wide track and everyone under that "umbrella" would get 100% total eclipse. We lived some 20.9738 miles from Portland, where the percentage of the event was set at about 95.1846%. *That's a pretty good number*, I thought. With the hype gaining fever pitch, I was entering the third circle of excitement, awaiting the big moment, forgetting the two massive storms that I just lived through. The eclipse was only two days away.

I was lucky enough to obtain two free pairs of solar eclipse sunglasses from my son. The special cardboard and plastic glasses "conform to and meet the transmission requirements of ISO 12312-2 filters for direct observation of the sun." Yeah buddy, no burnt retinas for me. I was ready. And my new cataract eye lens was safe.

According to the talking heads who seemed to be on every channel, they claimed that during the totality event, the corona would be larger than usual, the moon would appear larger, the darkening would look like nighttime, temperatures would drop some five to fifteen degrees, and the winds would be still. Sounded ominous to me. Even biblical. Like a two vodka and coke event.

I started tracking the path of totality at about 2 p.m.. At that time, I started my vigil in Carbondale, Illinois at 2:01, then Cleveland, Ohio at 3:15, then Buffalo, New York at 3:20, then Portland Maine at 3:31, the exact time they forecasted. I was outside at 3:10 with the wife, both of us staring into the sky with our special retina protecting eyewear, staring at the partially hidden sun. I could clearly see the crescent sun being slowly hidden by the moon. I was waiting to sight the "diamond ring" effect and the full corona of the sun. I was ready!

At the closest point of totality, the sun kept shining on Bauneg Beg Lake. The light diminished by 36.94378%. There was a slight temperature change, but no visual changes in the size of the sun or moon. Well, at 93,000,000 miles away, the sun always looks the same to me. The moon, more than 225,000 miles, so that looked normal too, at least through my special ISO glasses. The only noticeable change was that there was no wind, and all around us was deathly quiet. No rustling trees, no chirping birds, no screeching chipmunks or squirrels, no barking dogs... Just silence. Three minutes later, the whole thing was over. It got a little brighter as the sun shone down on the lake and warmed us once again. The news broadcasts gave us news from those places that were under the dome of doom. There, it was dark as night, and people were whooping and hollering and marveling at the extraordinary event they were witnessing. Some areas saw a temperature drop of fifteen degrees. People were beside themselves in awe of this phenomenon. Me, I was disappointed. It was not the big hoopla that was being hyped. It was two hours I could have spent cleaning my yard and working on my tan.

To be honest, I had more excitement from the two major snowstorms I had just lived through than this solar non-event. The next solar eclipse that will grace the state of Maine will be May 1, 2079. I doubt I'm here!

I may sell my ISO sunglasses for a tidy profit!

NOTE: For folks who were within the path of totality, the cell phone percentage usage dropped by 40% during that three to four-minute period of awe. Maine had projected some 15,000 visitors in the ski regions, but received about 50,000 visitors that helped boost the local economy. With a mediocre winter, the influx was badly needed. Sometimes, Mother Nature can be benevolent.

back it up some

It was a warm late spring day and the beginning of the unofficial start of summer. Like every Memorial Day weekend, the lake faithful returned to beautiful Bauneg Beg Lake after a long winter, ready to open their summer residences and get their waterfronts looking like marinas with their boats, jet skis, fishing boats, paddle boards, and every other type of watercraft you could imagine.

For me, the best part of the season is sitting on my front deck, overlooking the boat launch anticipating the coming antics, guffaws, and miscellaneous tomfoolery that was sure to happen, whether intended or not. It doesn't take long, when sooner or later I hear a boat trailer come rattling down the boat ramp with its prized possession on the back, ready to meet the water for another year.

Recently, a white pickup truck backed an 18-foot bow rider into the shallow boat ramp off of Corbin Way. I recognized the boat from years past, although the sailors were somewhat unfamiliar to me. Be it my age, or the vodka, made no difference, I suppose. Without getting out of the truck, they proceeded to back into the water without hesitation. My kind of guys. The truck stopped and came to rest with the four truck tires being halfway submerged in the water.

But... the boat trailer was still not in deep enough to float the heavy rig.

Popeye and Brutus (not their real names) got out of the truck and proceed into knee high water to the front of the boat. Not that the water was that high, but both men lifted their shorts up to their crotch as high as they could, exposing a leggy farmer's tan. You know what I mean, right? Popeye grabbed the front of the boat and started lifting it up and down while pushing, trying to persuade the long boat off the trailer. I could see the tires of the trailer were only half submerged, meaning they had to back out a little further. After several seconds of lifting, bouncing, and trying to move the boat, nothing happened. And his shorts kept falling to their normal length. Pulling his pants up again and asking Brutus for help, both of them again went through the same gyrations to no avail. I was talking to myself, saying, "Back it out a little, and it will float off by itself."

Both men stood back, looking over their dilemma. What to do, what to do? Suddenly, looking under the front of the trailer, low and behold, the strap from the winch to the boat was still attached. It took a minute to unhook the strap and free the boat. Not moving the truck, they again tried coaxing the boat backwards with sheer force. Nada! Not one inch. And their shorts unrolled to their regular length. Yeah, let's not get those shorts wet. It was time for me to get my favorite beverage and enjoy the show taking place nearby. And it was free!

Returning to my perch, and now with proper hydration in hand, the show continued. After several more attempts, trying to coax the boat off the trailer and refusing to move the truck backwards, they came up with another inventive plan. Using a nylon tie-down strap and turnbuckle, they hooked one end to the lower nose cleat on the boat and the other end to the side of the trailer. The idea was to crank the strap tight, forcing the boat backward, thus sliding the vessel off the trailer bunks. The dry trailer bunks. After several tries, that didn't work either. So they pulled up their falling shorts one more time and stood back, studying their dilemma. They seemed perplexed. I wanted to yell out, "Just back the truck up a few feet and it will float off by itself!" But what would the fun be in that? Learn by doing right?

It happened so fast I barely got a glimpse of the phantom bike rider. Out of nowhere, a third man came flying down the right of way on what looked like a 3/4 size adult two-wheel bike and, without stopping, rode it high speed into the shallow water of the ramp near the boat. I guess they were taking too long to get back to the cottage and their cavalry came to the rescue. The new arrival was in two feet of water and merely tossed the bike aside... underwater. All I could see was one handle bar sticking out of the water, marking its location. Popeye and Brutus didn't seem surprised at the new arrival. Now the three of them planned their attack to move the boat backwards and into the shallow waters of the lake. Popeye and Brutus hoisted their shorts one more time, but Bike Boy didn't bother. After several more attempts, it was Bike Boy that suggested to them to move the truck back a few feet.

Without hesitation, Brutus jumped in the truck cab and rolled the trailer back about five feet when the boat magically lifted off the trailer and floated calmly in the shallow ramp area. Soon, the boat motor was started and ran evenly when the helmsman gave the okay sign for the truck to leave. Bike Boy grabbed his two-wheeled bike from the water and hoisted it on the trailer for its ride home. Funny though, once the boat floated, their shorts stayed up around their crotch. Things sure are funny sometime.

All that work, and the answer was just five feet away.

some days...

A heavy torrential rain was pouring down hard over the driveway as I was getting ready to go out to the laundromat to get my weekly washing done. Yeah, having a broken-down washing machine for a month makes you appreciate it when the machine runs like it's supposed to.

Before heading out to clean my clothes, I had to make sure my furry house guest went to relieve himself, as I'd be gone for several hours. No sense leaving the critter home with a full bladder. I knew he wouldn't like going out in this heavy rain, but I had a schedule to keep, and I was going to keep it. As soon as we got outside, he tried clawing his way back to the house as quick as he could. We weren't out there one full minute when he was already soaking wet and shaking the water off as dogs do. I felt bad, but I didn't want to leave him knowing he might use the cottage as his personal toilet. (It's much more fun coming home to some wet dog smell on the furniture.) So, I dragged him to his outside pee-pee parlor only to find him crawling under the car in the carport and staying there. While I'm trying to coax him out from under the two-ton car, a large hornet's nest fell from its perch in the overhead of the portable garage, landing two feet from me. I didn't see any activity and nonchalantly kicked the large nest into the driveway and into monsoon rain. All of a sudden, the small flying stinging insects came out of the drenched nest looking for something or someone to take out their revenge. You could say they were as mad as a wet hornet. That's all it took to get the dog and me out of the garage and up the street. Seems we both had to relieve ourselves more than we thought. We finished our business before heading inside so the pooch could get toweled off and get a well-deserved treat. Me... I had very wet shoes. And I had to go... well, you know!

〜

We bought a new GMC Acadia in 2020. One of the features I enjoy most about the vehicle (which is so much smarter than I am) was the power tailgate. I could press the button on my remote (fob) and the tailgate lifted to the full open position, waiting for me to approach the rear with arms full of groceries, cases of water, clean laundry, or whatever, and it opens like magic from a long way off.

One day I was kidding with She-Who-Must-Be-Obeyed about the gate and how I loved the wireless feature. I told her that it would be funny if I opened the gate from afar just as someone, unbeknownst to them, didn't see the gate lift, and the door would catch them in the head or neck. While I thought that was funny, the better half scolded me and said something about acting my age. Sometimes I don't think she really knows me. But every week that we did groceries, I would tell her, "I hope someone's coming by the back of the car." Then I would hit the fob and open the gate to see if I could catch anyone. In reality, I would have felt bad if anything so sinister would happen to some unaware person. Hey, that could have been my mother or father, or some other loved one. But still, the thought was there. Of course, it never happened, but for some reason, it was always in the back of my mind.

Now that you know the backstory, let me tell you what happened on the same day the hornet's nest came crashing down. Watch out what you wish for is a truism. How many times have you heard that saying? If you know me, you know I have issues with lack of karma, and a female inner child that does not like me. Over the years, she's proved it too many times, and this particular one-in-a-million event was all her fault. She's saying, "No, it wasn't." But I know she caused it.

I was placing the large bags of unlaundered clothes in the back of the SUV when the large door started coming down to the closed position. I had unintentionally pressed the button on my fob that was in my pants pocket, along with other items. I wasn't aware the door was closing on me, and as I straightened out, I caught the edge of the moving door on the side of my face, knocking off my Navy Veteran cap and moving my glasses to the side of my face. Yeah, it was a surprise, and it got my attention, but I didn't cry. I thought how this was an appropriate consequence for wanting this to happen to someone else. See... no karma and no inner child support. Not to worry, the SUV did not sustain any damage... yet!

~

Recently, I took my furry house guest on a road trip to the local bank so he could whine, bark, tremble, and shake until the nice lady at the drive-thru sent a treat out for the little monster. Grabbing it from me like he hadn't eaten in two weeks, he proceeded to crumble the little milk bone into tiny fragments on the seat for me to clean later. Thank you Mutt, thank you!

Having completed my financial transaction, it was time to head home. Traveling south on Route 4 from the bank was a nice country drive that takes one over some gradual hilly roadways, making the drive somewhat scenic and peaceful, with no cares in the world.

I was coming down a small hilly section when I noticed a very large bird with a very wide wingspan floating high above in the windstream. The road was tree lined on both sides and as I was traveling south down the road, the large bird was traveling north some 200 feet over the highway. Just the two of us, like passing ships in the night. Only it was late morning.

All of a sudden, a large swath of poop came flying towards the ground. I guess the bird really had to go. If I'm traveling south at 55 mph, and the bird is traveling north at whatever speed large birds fly at, then what were the chances that a large sticky, light-colored glob of bird residue would hit my windshield, dead center of the viewing range? For most people, it would have been a miss. For me, 100%, because the bird had help from my inner child. Hard to believe. I think the splatter was as wide as the bird's wingspan. Just another day in paradise. I was glad to get home on the beautiful shores of Bauneg Beg Lake.

"Honey, I think you need to clean your windshield!"

must be the weather

The winter weather was some of the worst the northern states had seen in over a decade. While we enjoyed a calm and warm January, we were fooled into thinking this would be a short winter season with little to no snow. Of course, when February came around, it roared in like a freight train going downhill with no brakes. On February 2nd, also known as Groundhog Day, I watched the local news to see what the famous rodent, Punxsutawney Phil, would predict for the rest of the winter. In short, his forecast said that if it could snow in hell, we were in for it. Six long weeks of excessive freezing cold, heavy snow, strong howling winds and head banging misery. So, I looked into my vodka reserves and settled in for what was to come. And... it did.

Living on a lake has its advantages and disadvantages. I live on the east side shore of a lake with the prevailing winds blowing into the front sliders nearly nonstop. We endured weeks of well below average cold, snow and wind during February. So, it was obvious to me that if I have issues with the winter weather, the critters around here will too. But, where do they go when the temperatures drop and they can't get to their nuts? Yeah, you guessed it... my cellar.

One day, when the wind was just short of blowing my hat off my balding pate, I thought I'd go visit my cellar and make sure everything was okay, especially in the pump room. It was the home of my water pump and hot water heater and the warmest area of the cellar. The room was built into the ground and was insulated to protect the plumbing. However, I could see that the little beasts had left their thanks by leaving me small pellets of poo as a gift for the use of my cellar to keep warm. Little heathens!

Years ago, I bought two Havahart traps to control these little crap machines. They were making a mess of my cellar, leaving droppings wherever they wanted. How rude, right? It was time to dust off the cages and put them back to work. So, armed with the two traps, some yummy peanut butter, and some choice Georgia peanuts, I set the traps in the cellar and waited.

Two days later, I returned to the cellar and, sure enough, both cages had tripped and in each trap was a mouse. They looked cute and frightened, yet the peanut butter and peanuts were gone, and there was a small amount of droppings under the cage. Since I had trapped them using these *compassionate* cages, I was at a loss at what to do with them. I didn't really want to kill them then have to explain to the wife what I had done. She would understand, but she wouldn't approve. So now what?

In the previous two weeks, we had been through two very large snowstorms. Across the street were large mounds of snow the city plow had pushed up along the roadside. Thinking I'd give the little critters a break, I walked across the street, up the four-foot high snow pile, and released the little furry crap factories on the ice covered snow, where they scampered away into the woods. Not once did they look back to thank me! Ungrateful little beasts! I returned to the shed, reloaded the two traps, and set them in the cellar to *hunt* for another day or two.

Two days later, and since I was outside, I decided to revisit the cellar and check on the cages. Again, both cages were tripped and in each cage were two more mice. Using the same procedure as before, I took them across the street and released them over the snowbank, where they scurried away. One of the mice ran about 20 feet and suddenly laid down on his side on the ice covered snow as if he died. I threw some chunks of snow at him, landing within close proximity, but he never moved. As I walked back to the shed and halfway up the driveway, I turned to look at the little guy, when all of a sudden, he stood up, looked at me (I think he was laughing), and ran off like he had pulled a fast one on me. With two days of capture and release, I reloaded the two traps to hunt for another day... or two.

Two days later, I went back to the cellar to check the two traps. Sure enough, both cages were again occupied with the unwanted vermin. *How many rodents lived under here?* I thought. I removed the cages and went to the shed to empty and reload the cages for another round. It had snowed lightly during the night before, and the driveway and grounds had a light cover of white fluffy snow that would melt itself away by afternoon. I crossed the street, climbed the snowbank, and emptied the two cages, watching the little critters scurry along into the woods, and went back to do the reloading process and return the cages to the cellar once again.

On leaving the cellar, I thought I'd check the roadside mailbox since we hadn't received mail in three days. Walking down the driveway, I suddenly slipped on the snow covered ice on the driveway, my feet going out from under me, and finding myself in a horizontal position (like I was being levitated), I came crashing down on my back, slamming the back of my head on the frozen ice covered hot top. I instantly grabbed my head, waiting for what I thought sure would be a bloody mess. I could only see white under my eyelids. I had never lost consciousness, but this was close. My glasses were on my chin, my Navy ball cap went flying three feet behind me, and my left jaw snapped out of joint. As I lay there trying to figure out if I was seeing angels or not, I found that I was not bleeding, but knew I was going to have a pounding headache. Then, I saw him!

While I'm lying there in my winter misery, I saw a little furry rodent run across the street and up my driveway, passing within ten feet of where I lay. I think he looked at me while running by, smiled, and kept running toward the house. Really? Was I seeing things? Was he a mirage? Did I hit my head that hard?

I crawled over to the fence to leverage my torso off the frozen driveway and put my glasses back on. I went to retrieve my ball cap and noticed the snow hidden ice slick that sent me flying. I readjusted my left jaw, snapping it back into place. I could see the tiny paw prints in the snow leading into the garage. Yep, mousy was back! But was I ready? Would I ever be ready? I'd been outsmarted by the local wildlife so many times in the past. Maybe all this wasn't worth the effort. Maybe!

I felt like I was on the TV show *Survivor* and I was losing. I was being outplayed, outwitted, and outlasted by a two-ounce critter who kept voting me out at the Tribal Council. I wonder if Jeff Probst ever had this feeling.

I'd go check the cellar, but I have a wicked headache!

NOTE: It was several days later, and my catch and release system was still underway. I didn't give up that easily, and I was maintaining my compassionate method of letting them go, unharmed, away from the house. What a sucker, huh?

I had caught another small reptile in the Havahart cage. As was now my standard operating procedure, I brought the cage with me and up the road, releasing the little bacteria-filled vermin in a field, thinking this would surely disorient the creature. Instead of running away like all the others, he just stayed there, peering at me with those little, dark, beady eyes. I walked toward him, thinking he'd scurry away, but no chance. He stood his ground. I tried some minor intimidation, only to be stared down. Really mouse?

I left him where he sat and walked home. Looking back, I couldn't see where he was just seconds before. It was another 75 feet to my driveway, and I started walking up toward the gambrel to put more yummy peanut butter in the trap and place it in the cellar for another round.

As I was opening the shed doors, I saw the little mouse come running up the driveway, across the mulched lawn toward the house. He followed me home. I knew it wouldn't be long before I'd see him again in the cage. Was it the cold weather? Maybe he liked the yummy peanut butter. Whatever it was, it seemed he was continuing to smart, outwit, and outplay me.

I'd never make it on *Survivor*!

I need to go buy more peanut butter! And vodka!

what was i thinking?

I t was another beautiful but hot day on the shores of Bauneg Beg Lake. Unlike last season, when we endured one of the rainiest summers in recorded history, this year we were living with one of the hottest summers ever recorded, especially for July. We were averaging 95 degrees each day with high humidity. By the end of the third week of July, we were getting reports that the high heat was about to end, and we would be getting back to more seasonal temperatures. At least for a while. Which ended up being a really good forecast, as we had the annual Family Gathering on an upcoming weekend. And the weather looked promising. Every year, I usually stress over the weather and drive the wife crazy with my intentions to change date, cancel the whole thing, or move to Canada. Not so this year. I was stress free... yeah, no!

One early morning, I was sitting at the kitchen table enjoying a cup of joe, contemplating all the things that I had on my list in preparation for the family outing.

Suddenly, out of the blue, I heard bells ringing. (With my tinnitus, it's really not that unusual for me.) I opened my phone, being sure it was a *Words with Friends* buddy making a move. Then I heard it again, so I opened my computer to see which hacker was bidding me a good morning before asking me for a ransom. But not today! Then the bell rang again. Looking out toward the back door, I saw a person walking near the entrance. At 8:30 in the morning?

At least the source of the bell was solved. So I went out to meet the stranger. He was dressed in work clothes, with a greenish reflective vest that one would see on a highway crew. He came toward me, shook my hand, and started in on his spiel.

Unknown Guy: (UG going forward) "Hi, I noticed your driveway is a little dried up. When was the last time you sealed it?"

Me: "I had it done a couple of years ago." Who the heck is this guy?

UG: "I can sealcoat your driveway for you, and I'll do a great job. I've been doing this work for thirty years and I'll do a good job for you. You won't be sorry."

I had this project on my to do list for late August or September, yet here was a guy with his son in tow scrounging up work.

Me: "Well, I did have the work on my list for later this year. Do you want to give me an estimate for the work?"

He does a quick survey of the driveway and walkway.

UG: "I can do the work for $500."

I thought to myself, *$500 is a third of the cost of the last guy I hired.*

Me: "You'll do the work for $500 and include both driveways and the walkway?"

UG: "Yes, and you'll be very happy with the final product, I promise you."

We shook hands over the $500 deal that I was hoping would still be agreeable come the fall. Then it all took another twist I wasn't expecting.

Me: "When do you want to schedule the work? Got any idea what your workload looks like?"

UG: "I'm going to do it right now. I have my son here and the truck has all I need. I'll be done in two hours, and you'll be very happy with the job, I promise. And I'm not spraying it. I'll hand trowel the entire area and seal the edges, too. There'll be no overspray."

Me: "What?"

UG: "Yeah, right now. This work is better done on really hot days like this, so the moisture in the sealer evaporates quicker and you can use your driveway by tonight... guaranteed."

Me: "Okay then, have at it. I'll move my cars out of the way.

Not talking to the wife first, I jumped on this deal before UG changed his mind. I was walking back to the house feeling like the cat that just ate the canary, thinking that this was going to be a good karma day. I rarely had those. Well, unless bad karma counts. Here I was getting a project done two months early and at a 60% cost saving from the previous time.

Soon, the two men were out there with large push brooms and a gas leaf blower, cleaning the entire expanse of the paved area to be treated. I was a very happy camper. I'd be the envy of Javica Lane.

While the boys were here laboring on a hot day, the wife and I left for a few hours. We had errands to run. So, before leaving, I paid UG our agreed to amount, and included a very generous tip for his promised good results. He was very happy and promised us a good job. We left for town, but I was already anxious to get back to see my newly resealed driveway. I was hoping for the best. I didn't know, or had ever heard of UG Paving, and here I was working on blind faith.

On our return, I was giddy coming down Javica Lane. Like a school boy on the last day of school before summer vacation with a marginal report card, but still making it to the sixth grade. Yeah, those were good years. But I digress.

As we approached the driveway, UG was gone but left behind a long length of barrier tape across the entire expanse of the work area. Just as he promised, UG and his son had trimmed back all the edges of the tarred area, sealed all the edges, provided a square and straight line of sealer, covered the entire area evenly, and the driveway looked terrific. UG had kept his word and provided a sound product that he said I'd be happy with. I was. Thank you, UG.

It was later in the day when the wife asked me. "Did you forget that the septic tank truck will be here in the morning?" I had forgotten about the behemoth truck weighing countless tons that would arrive and use my newly sealed driveway to pump two years of waste from my holding tank. It was late afternoon, and I thought about calling the company to delay the work for a couple of weeks. I decided to let it ride and take my chances, since my karma was on the positive side. So, I poured myself a refreshing beverage and hoped for the best. Yeah, that truck would make a mess on my newly sealed driveway. I never thought of that the day before. Of course, I was taken by surprise, but that's just an excuse. What was I thinking?

I figured the tank might get pumped later in the day and it would give the sealer some twenty-four hours or better to harden up.

The following day, it was on my mind as I sat at the table, nursing a cup of coffee, wondering what the day would bring. It was before 8 a.m. that I heard the truck's air-brakes stop in front of my driveway and saw the driver looking at the barrier tape. It was time to face the music. Was I in for good karma or bad karma? My inner child was quiet. What's wrong with her, anyway? And why was the truck here so darned early?

I went out to meet the driver, and I told him I'd remove the barrier tape so he could back into the driveway.

STG: (Septic Tank Guy). "I'm not backing up in the driveway. It's too new and the truck will leave marks all over it."

Me: "Can you reach the tank ninety-five feet away from here?"

STG: "Yeah I can. I have enough hose on the truck."

However, looking around, we decided to back into my neighbor's adjacent driveway and run the hoses across my lawn to the tank, and that worked great for him and me. Best part is that he recognized the newly sealed area and didn't want to upset it. Or me! Nice guy, huh?

STG: "I have to ask you, though. If you knew we were coming today, why would you sealcoat your driveway yesterday?"

Me: "It was a spur of the moment, unplanned kind of thing. The guy showed up at my door, offered me a great price for a job I had on my fall schedule, and was ready to do the work right then. Never had to wait for the work. So I jumped on it. My wife reminded me that you were coming today."

STG: "Looks like it all worked out then."

The Septic crew even made sure NOT to let the hose couplings drag on the newly sealcoated areas where the hose rested during pumping. Thoughtful. While pumping, the head guy asked me if I'd had minor issues with back up lately. We, in fact, had issues for the past two weeks or so, which I found peculiar that he would ask that.

Me: "How would you know that?"

STG: "I can see telltale signs of solid discharge from the outflow pipe. Can you go flush the toilet for me a couple of times to make sure the piping is cleared out while I'm here?"

So, off I went and did the required flushing. When I returned, he had the suction hose up against the overflow pipe, sucking out any residual butt nappy debris that might be lingering in the dark recesses of the septic system. How lucky was I to have an energetic guy willing to ensure the system was working at 100% before leaving? He and his associate (Septic Tank Guy Associate), made sure to pick up the hose at the couplings and left the site as if they were never there.

Looking back on the last twenty-four hours, my karma was on a positive high note. I wasn't used to that. Usually, my inner child (who lives in me rent free), always finds ways to mess with me. In one day, I got my tarred areas resealed perfectly, and my septic system maintained by some very thoughtful and helpful *friends*.

Yeah, life is good on the shores of beautiful Bauneg Beg Lake.

boat ramp shenanigans

It was a bright sunny afternoon on the shores of the beautiful lake I called home. And also the end of a July two-week stint for vacationers from near and far, and to be truthful, watching their boats leave the lake always warmed my heart. Or was that the vodka?

On this particular occasion, I was sitting out on the deck enjoying the ambiance of the calm water, watching the sun sparkle and dance over the small waves rolling up on my beach. Looking out in the middle of Patriot Cove, I notice a 20-foot pontoon boat with two occupants. The boat's bow pointing at me, just sitting there. Soon, they pulled away and did a large circle, leaving a trail of white, foamy water before coming back to rest in the same place. I guess the slight breeze was keeping them off station. I thought for a minute they might be looking for me. Why? Well, I do wear many hats here. I'm on the Board of Trustees, I'm the Assistant Buoy Master, and I'm a local international book author, publishing stories like these. It ended up being none of those, so my feeling of self-importance was a waste of time.

Soon, the boat started on another large turn before returning to its resting place in front of me. I was wondering what was going on.

It's not like there was much happening in our little corner of Patriot Cove. Then, for a third time, the boat made another large sweeping turn before coming back to rest near the same place on the water. I took my Mark 28, 1943, BUSHIPS, Navy Bridge binoculars to check out the occupants. A man and a woman were both still looking my way... or near me.

Then, the lovely wife and first mate of the boat *Hope Floats* says, "There's a truck up on the road trying to back a trailer down the ramp road, but he's facing the opposite direction. Instead of the truck facing up the road, it's facing down the road toward the dead end."

That put an end to the mystery of the circling pontoon boat. Most, if not all, trucks and trailers that use the ramp access road usually find a nearby driveway to turn their rigs around and face a more southerly direction to ease their long trailers down the ramp road at about a 30-degree angle, unencumbered, easily straightening out the long boat carriers and continue slowly down the road to the waters' edge. This had to be the first time for this guy.

By facing the opposite direction from the norm, he had to back *up* the hilly tree covered lane and swing the trailer around a road sign-post, avoid a mailbox and a ditch and a fir tree that were on private property. Oh yeah, and the angle of the turn from the Lane onto the ramp road was more than 120.08593 degrees. Making it nearly impossible given the narrowness of the road entry from that angle. However, having a few beers might have helped the driver in his quest to achieve the impossible. There's no way he would attempt this sober. Soon, it became obvious he had imbibed a little during the day. Miraculously, he did manage to get the 24-foot trailer down the road, stopping at the edge of the water. It was a first for me. I had to get a cold beverage because I knew this was going to get even better. I wasn't disappointed.

As the driver got out of the truck, the pontoon came closer. The pontoon driver called out, "Put the trailer in the water!" The slurred response came from Truck Guy, "Oh yeah, okay." The trailer was backed into what I thought was a pretty good depth, with the long carpeted bunks barely above the rippling water. Then the pontoon driver made his first attempt to mount the trailer. A slight breeze pushed him sideways, forcing him to back off and try again.

He backed out into the Cove further than he needed to, and came in to give it another try, again being forced off by the breeze. Truck Guy was in the water between the truck and trailer, trying to free the long nylon winch lanyard they would need to clip to the front of the boat and haul it onto the trailer. Now, having backed out for a third try, Boat Guy again went out a ways to try another run. It seems that when he got close to the trailer he would put his motor in neutral, thinking he would glide the pontoon on the trailer. I love that stuff, because it never works, ever. And, of course, the wind blew him sideways, fouling another valiant attempt.

Then this conversation:

Truck Guy: "Maybe I should move the trailer and straighten it out."

Boat Guy: "No, it's okay. I'll make another try. I should get on, it's the wind."

Truck Guy: Mumbled something I couldn't hear. I think he was drooling.

The pontoon backed off again for a fourth try and again managed to get foiled by the breeze. Without further dialogue, Truck Guy got in his vehicle and drove the trailer backwards into the water another five feet. Lake water was now edging the truck's rocker panels, and the trailer bunk pads were barely visible from my perch. He certainly was deep enough, but Boat Guy wasn't impressed. Now he couldn't see the bunks really well, left with only the trailer winch to line up on.

Despite Boat Guys' irritation, Truck Guy exited the cab, came to the back of the truck now in deeper water, and promptly laid down on the tonneau cover with his feet dangling over the tailgate. I guess he was tired.

Remember at the beginning I mentioned there were two people on the pontoon? There was a nice lady onboard who had remained quiet throughout this whole event, probably wishing she had stayed back at the cottage.

Before making another unprecedented fifth and sixth approach to the now sunken trailer, Boat Guy suggested that Truck Guy get in the water and grab the boat's front rails on the next approach and help guide the 20-foot vessel onto the trailer bunks. That request urged the lady into action as well.

As the pontoon approached the trailer, the lady decided to go overboard in what she assumed was shallow water. From where the truck was sitting, it might have been a good assumption. But not here on this ramp. She got on the front end of the pontoon and lowered herself into the water. Not feeling the bottom right away, she decided to let go, thinking she would land safely hip high in the warm waters of the ramp. As she entered the water, she actually disappeared from site, going completely underwater only to resurface, spitting out what had to be some foul tasting oil and gas filled water. As she stood, she was chest high in the cool waters of the ramp. Yuck! I hope she had a towel on the boat. She moved forward and Truck Guy decided to join her at the trailer wench. Both of them managed to get the boat fairly straight on the trailer.

NOTE: In the spirit of this year's Summer Olympics, I did give the lady a 9.5 mark for the water entry. I had to deduct minor points for unusual facial expressions and flailing arms on entry. The wind-milling wasn't pretty. I thought the 9.5 was generous.

Before getting the boat fully trailered, Boat Guy thought he'd help maneuver the boat forward by using his 75 HP outboard motor. He revved the boat until blue, smelly smoke permeated the area, killing any flying insects that might have been around. I think he wilted a pine tree too. Why? He had trimmed his motor out of the water. Idiot! At some point, the two people in the water managed to get the bow strap attached to the U-bolt on the front of the boat. Truck guy then cranked to boat onto the trailer until the bow reached the trailer's winch.

With the boat now on the trailer, Truck Guy slowly pulled the loaded trailer out of the water onto the ramp before stopping. It seemed the boat was not actually square on the trailer, but they had had enough for this day. After all, waiting for the truck for thirty minutes, seven attempts to load the boat, a near drowning, and using the motor to cause a bug-killing spree was enough action for one day.

I'm sure Truck Guy found leaving the ramp road was much easier than getting onto it. God, I love this place. Now, where's that beverage?

being neighborly

t was a bright sunny morning on the shores of beautiful Bauneg Beg Lake. There was a slight breeze and the two flags were rippling in the early morning breeze some 15 feet above the boat docks. It was the typical scene I saw every morning giving thanks to God for the gift of living in such a wonderful place.

I was just sitting down to enjoy a hot cup of coffee when I heard what can only be described as a woodchipper trying to grind a Buick. Yeah, it was that ear splitting. It was only 7:30 a.m., so that couldn't be it. I got up to see what the strange racket was about and soon saw the nuisance. A nearby neighbor was trying to back out his pontoon boat from the dock into shallow Patriot Cove.

The neighbor had recently purchased a used 16-foot pontoon boat, and the vessel had been sitting on the dock for about a week without being used. I thought that was strange given that most people who get a new water sled put 2,8873,973 miles on it the first day and have a Saudi Arabian gas tanker parked in their driveway. Not this neighbor. The only action was in trying to get the main canopy up in place, then it sat there for a week. Maybe he was a responsible boat owner and wanted to pay the high cost of registration, get a milfoil sticker, and the proper boaters' insurance. No matter, I'm going with that.

The day before, the neighbor took the boat out for the first time on his own. The show included a dizzying attempt to get the boat away from the dock. I guess just backing out into the cove wasn't fun enough. After some difficult close to shore maneuvering, he finally got boat pointing in the right direction and head out slowly for his maiden cruise. After more than an hour and a half, the little boat returned to the dock. Hampered by a small breeze, the neighbor slowly, very slowly, excruciatingly slowly, approached the dock and promptly tapped the front corner of the dock. There was no damage, as it amounted to no more than a love tap. With some manly determination, he got onto the dock and, after a few hard minutes, he managed to strong arm the little boat back in place along the aluminum dock. In all honesty, I had to give the neighbor credit for managing his first lake voyage alone.

And here we were again. He was going out for another trip around the pond in the early morning hours. So, being an expert sailor, a former member of the United States Navy, and having in my possession a Navy certification card as a qualified helmsman for an aircraft carrier, I thought I should go out and offer my support and recommendations to the neighbor to better use and enjoy his new second-hand ride. But still, what the heck was that earsplitting noise?

Seeing him depart from his dock and pointing the boat's bow in my direction, I thought it was time to go outside and see if I could help him. Would he even want my help? We had not been close neighbors, but it was time to step up and be the neighbor I needed to be. So I committed myself to be friendly no matter what came of it. From the top of my deck, we made eye contact, and I waved him over to the front of my docks so I could offer my tutorial on boat handling.

I strode down the twelve steps from the deck to the wooden walkway that extended to the aluminum dock. Having waterproofed the wood decking the day before, it had a nice shine on it, largely due to the light rain that had fallen during the night. It was a little tacky and my sneakers didn't slide well on the newly stained decking.

On my second step forward, I went down on the decking like a giant tree falling. I hit the deck at my full 6-foot height, touching little on the way down. That was embarrassing, to say the least.

In my semi-conscious state, I was laying completely stretched out on the four-foot wide deck, hands at my side like I fell at attention. I was facing to my right, quickly assessing any physical damage and thinking, *Gee, I think my lawn needs cutting!* What the heck is wrong with me? I dropped like a 225 pound weight, at attention, probably traumatized myself, and I'm thinking the grass needs a trim? Really?

When I was younger, I would have sprung up like nothing happened to avoid any semblance of embarrassment. Not today. I was looking for my glasses and my fake front tooth. Talk about a freak show!

Neighbor: "Are you okay?"

Me: "Yeah, I'm fine. I'm seventy-five, and I fall all the time."

As he approached the dock, I'm certain he saw that my T-shirt was wet from sucking up all the rain that had fallen on the deck that I tried cleaning up. However, little more was said about my fall. I changed the subject back to the boat and the noise it was making. I knew right away what it was. The motor trim was too high, and the propeller was barely in the water. I was guessing the newest lake mariner needed some tutorial on boat operation and management.

As he approached, I had to bend over to push the front end of the pontoon out a few inches before hitting my dock and bringing the boat and him to an abrupt halt. I had done that once to The First Mate on my pontoon boat that sent her bouncing from bench to bench like a pinball before landing harmlessly on the deck. But I digress. With the boat safely alongside, I showed him why the boat was not only making the grinding noise, but why yesterday's lake cruise took an hour longer than it should have. I explained that the propeller was almost out of the water and that he needed to trim the motor down to lower the prop for smoother and proper operation.

Me: "Look on your T handle. There should be a small black lever to lower and raise your propeller. Move it downward and it should put the lower unit deeper in the water. The boat will drive easier, sound quiet, and travel at a much better rate of speed. Snail is not a speed."

Neighbor: "Oh, okay." Then promptly complied, placing the motor in the right position.

By now, I'm starting to feel a little trauma in both my wrists and my right knee. I pushed the boat off the dock and into the shallow depths of Patriot Cove, a happy new lake sailor motoring around the lake like a pro. Well, it'll come.

On the way back up to the house, I noticed the dry spot and somewhat of an outline of where I fell. It was time to change my T-shirt too! Was it too early for a cold vodka and Coke? I should say not!

Best of all, I had taken the first step at reaching out to the neighbor as a friend. It was well accepted on both sides. Sometimes the most important things in life is being an unlikely friend. I heard once that the best vitamin for a Christian is be one (B1).

How true is that? I'm having that drink anyway.... Hey, I have trauma!

tidbits

T ime was passing quickly during late summer on beautiful Bauneg Beg Lake. After what seemed like an endless summer of ninety plus humid degrees, the weather was finally returning to more comfortable levels, and life on the lake was again more tolerable. Well, most of the time. It seems that sometimes you wonder what and why things happen like they do. For instance, here are a couple of head-scratching, sphincter-tightening, bowel-emptying (too much?), events that I had to endure recently. The *why* was beyond me.

SPIDERS

It was a warm day, and I was getting ready to get some house upgrades done by my local friendly contractor. I knew some of the work would involve removing a cellar window and a partial wall. To help clear the stored clutter, I decided to go into the cellar and relocate the summer items that might be in his way. As I made the corner to enter the area under the main deck where the doors were, I walked straight into an unseen spider web that stretched the whole six-foot wide area of the entrance. I was instantly covered across my head and shoulders in a wet slimy mass of thin webbing, making my skin crawl in disgust. I didn't know that a big person, such as myself, could move as fast as I did. I started swearing in foreign tongues and heard my inner child laughing with joy. What the heck is wrong with her?

Once I regained some sense of control, I scraped off the unseen gooey mess and silenced my inner child. I had the urge to go change my shirt, feeling assaulted by the unseen arachnid. I do not suffer from arachnophobia, but being covered in wet slime could push me over the edge.

Since I was already covered, I thought I might as well complete the job I came down here to do. I opened the large, heavy wood doors and walked directly into another unseen, large body-covering web that encased my head and shoulders, draping the now fallen web over my arms. I quickly reacted to remove whatever slimy threads I could find off of me. I needed a shower really soon. As I completed relocating any contractor interference, I went to check on my water pump while I was in the area. And there, on the ceiling, looking down at me and squirming to find safe shelter, was a spider the size of a half dollar. It was a water spider, and he was HUGE. By now, my mental acuity is nonexistent. I'd had enough. Three encounters with the Spiders from Hell was enough for one day. Yeah, time for a shower, change of clothes and a much needed, nerve-calming, vodka and Coke on ice. A tall one!

SPIDER TWO

The next day I had another encounter with the eight-legged, creepy, evasive, but slow-moving arachnid. It seemed like my lack of karma was continuing. Still, I needed to be on my way to a Lowe's store to pick up materials. I thought I'd use the wife's GMC Acadia and proceeded to the portable garage and hit the road. Turning from the driveway into the open vinyl rolled up door of the portable shelter, I was immediately covered in another wet, slimy, and HUGE web that encompassed my head and shoulders down to my arms. How big could these webs get? I was acting like a man who was going into some neurotic fit. If anyone was watching my gyrations, wild arm movements, and heard me speaking in tongues (I never know what language it is), they might have thought it an unlikely place to practice the Watusi, the Twist, the Mashed Potato, or some other 60s dance fad. NOTE: If you don't know what those are, you probably weren't born in the 60s.

Having been through this event days earlier, I regained my composure and quickly scraped off the thin, wet veils of thread that I could feel. I still felt *covered* but I was relatively certain I had removed most of the offending web. I was already planning another cold beverage once I returned home. At this point, I'll have the vodka folks working two shifts. Why do I feel itchy?

SPIDER THREE

It was within the same week that I had a third encounter with the eight-legged terror. The wife and I decided to take a pontoon ride around the lake and relax from a long week. Usually, the one-hour cruise around the pond relaxed us as we admired the sights and sounds of water and fowl... and the noisy, speeding, uncaring boaters who might be out there with us.

I got on the boat and started to unsnap the seat covers. As I finished, I went to bend over the rail to untie the boat from the cleat. Again, not seeing the wet slimy web, I bent over and got covered head first, over my head, down my shoulders and arms. God, how big do these things get? Again, I reacted like a man having a fit. Not sure what language I was cussing in. Was I a web magnet or what? This web was so big, it stretched all the way to the outboard motor housing. I wonder if God forgives you when you curse in a language you don't know. I hope so. Either way, I'm having a drink when I get home.

BOAT #2

It was a warm early evening when my cell phone pinged alerting me to a new message coming in. A local neighbor had posted on Facebook (where the truth can always be found) that a small bumper boat was stuck in the weeds, and the author was looking for its owner. Well, not many residents on the lake own bumper boats that one would find and enjoy at a carnival or amusement park. Of course, as luck would have it, I knew who the owner was and where the little runaway boat belonged. So, being part of the lake commission on water safety, I felt an obligation to go retrieve the little motorized rubber boat and haul it back to its resting place. I replied on Facebook (where the truth can always be found) that I was going to go salvage the runaway motorized tube. I was hoping I wouldn't be attacked by the spider web from hell in the process.

Cruising down the east side of the lake, we found the little round boat stuck in some thick weeds in Statuto Cove (not a real named cove, but it could be one day). The First Mate and I approached the derelict vessel and promptly tied a rope around a chrome rail and hauled it out of the thicket. The water was shallow for my 65 hp outboard, but we made the transition easily. Now in open water, I made a more secure knot in the line and tied it off the back rail of the pontoon. It was surprisingly heavy for a small, fun boat. We made it back to the owner's dock, where I tied the vessel to the dock posts with several half hitches and made sure the boat would stay in place until the owner arrived at some point. Boat #2 was safely in place... for now.

A few days later, we decided to take an evening ride around the pond so I could check on all nine lake buoys, ensuring they were all on station, keeping us safe from low shoals. As we rode down the west side of the lake, The First Mate noted that she couldn't see the little Boat #2 at the dock, and the owner had in fact NOT come back to his cottage yet. So, where was Boat #2? Taking a hard turn of the helm in an easterly direction, we headed straight for the dock. As expected, the little boat was nowhere in sight. How could it have escaped the Houdini knots I used to secure it? That was baffling. I looked in the water near the dock, but the 20 feet of 3/8th twisted white nylon line was nowhere to be seen. Maybe it was still attached to the boat. We continued with our search and rescue mission.

Cruising down the same side of the lake as the previous time, we again found the little Boat #2 in the same thicket off shore as it was the first time we recovered it. I looked for the rope once again, but found no signs of it. I found it hard to believe that BOTH knots loosened and fell off the little vessel. How could that happen? The First Mate thought it might be sabotage at first. It would be hard to prove. I didn't care, I just had to get it out of the shallow area again. So we backed it out into Statuto Cove once again and pulled Little #2 to the back of the pontoon to secure another rope to the rear rail and hauled it back to its home.

When I got it in position at the rear of the pontoon boat, I used my docking line and fashioned a nautical figure 8 knot using both lines. As soon as I tied the slip-proof knot, it slid apart and the tow line fell into the water, allowing little Boat #2 to drift off on its own. So, I maneuvered the pontoon boat for several minutes, trying to get in a good place to catch the boat and retie it for towing. After several tries, and glares from The First Mate, I caught the boat and finally had it tied to the rear of the pontoon boat. Boat #2 was sure measuring up to be a handful.

Within a few minutes, we had cruised back to its home dock. This time, another neighbor was there to take charge of Boat #2 and place it back in the harness area alongside Boat #12. He would let the owner know of the second escape and capture of runaway Boat #2. For now, the recovery mission was complete and time for... well, you know!

Only time would tell if the little Boat #2 would try another Houdini escape. God, I love this place!

the smallest
boat ever

I t was a warm day on the lake and there hadn't been much activity on the boat ramp in the past few days. It's my source of enjoyment, as you know. However, on one particular morning, a peculiar launch took place. It was the smallest boat and motor combination I'd ever seen on the lake. There was a young man with his father (I assume), and they had a small trailer hauling the little boat to the ramp.

The little boat brought to mind those little kiddie boats you see at fairs or amusement parks that toddlers would enjoy, envisioning themselves on the high seas and sailing around the world. Or is some cases, just crying and wanting the ride to stop. The boat was no more than 6 feet long and 3 feet wide and sported a 15 hp motor attached to the transom. The motor housing looked to be a throwback to the 70s, but I couldn't really tell. *What an odd combination*, I thought.

The son and dad lifted the boat off the trailer and set it on the surface of the water, where it floated in all its glory. I couldn't believe how small this boat was and the young man was nearly six feet tall. He climbed into the little boat and towered over it as he sat in the one seat center section. It even had a steering wheel in it. I figured that somewhere along the way, they installed the dash and motor on their own, creating this unusual craft.

Soon, the young man started pulling the start cord and after several tries, the motor coughed to life and ran... well... it ran. As he started to pull away from the ramp, the motor stalled and the pulling started again. And that went on for several minutes until he got the motor at a high idle and put it in gear and the little boat roared out onto the lake, looking like a speck on the water as compared to similar larger boats. I got my Navy Bridge Binoculars to watch the action. The young man was towering over the small craft, seemingly out of balance.

Over the next several days, I saw the little boat out on the lake. Most of the time, the young man was alone, and other times, he had a smaller passenger. It must have been tight sitting quarters. Often time, the motor would stall, and I would see him yank on the starter cord until it would eventually start again. Sometimes, I'd see him paddling his little boat as the tired little motor wouldn't start. Then, later, the motor was running again. The young man seemed to enjoy his trips around the lake, staying away from the bigger boats and heavy wave action. But here's the real story:

- His little boat was registered and had a milfoil sticker.
- He wore a life jacket every time he went out.
- He stayed away from the shoreline.
- He had safety gear onboard the little boat.

That is one responsible young man and very welcomed here on Bauneg Beg Lake. And his little boat, too!

the boat ramp

One of my greatest joys in these retirement years is sitting on the front deck of the cottage overlooking the pristine waters of beautiful Bauneg Beg Lake. Sitting on my perch, visitors wouldn't be surprised to find me reading my favorite novelist and sipping a cold beverage on a hot day. And typically, on most days, I am assured of being entertained by people's shenanigans, faux pas, tomfoolery and other mishaps that occur only 100 feet away on the private boat ramp at the end of Corbin Way. I wonder if folks know I have a ringside seat. Here are a couple of recent boat ramp tidbits for you.

STORY ONE

It was a happy time of the season for me. Lake visitors and renters were starting to go home after their entitled vacation on the lake. Using the well-known, although private boat ramp, they would now be removing their gas-guzzling, noise-making, smoke-generating, mosquito-killing water sleds. What they saw as yachts were just everyday boats of different sizes and construction.

As I was sitting quietly, wondering how many Russians it took to squeeze enough potatoes to make a gallon of good vodka, I was brought out of my reverie by conflicting noises. One was a yellow and white two-seat jet boat coming around Windy Way Point into Patriot Cove. The small speed boat bobbed on the water as the operator looked pointedly towards the ramp road, wondering where her trailer was. Soon, noise number two, I mean the trailer, was backing down the road, followed by an SUV of sorts. Usually, folks use pickup trucks, but not today. Obviously visitors!

The driver backed into the shallow water of the ramp, stopping near the water's edge, leaving the trailer three-quarters submerged with the dry carpeted bunk rails showing above water. The boat was waved over to the left side of the boat trailer where the man was soon standing. I thought the lady driver would mount the trailer and get the boarding process started, but no!

She coasted in, slowed, and then started to walk to the front of the jet boat, looking for a way to get off. He was holding on to the front of the boat, standing in less than two feet of water.

Her: "I don't want to get my legs and feet wet."

Him: "Okay, but how are you going to get off? I don't want you putting the boat on the trailer, and one of us has to be out here to grab it."

Note: I'd seen the boat removal process many times, but I was confused why this guy wouldn't let his better half put the boat on the trailer while she was right there in the boat at the rear of the trailer. Why not let her do it since he was right there in the water at the winch? Did he not let her drive the boat to the ramp? Maybe she couldn't back the trailer down Corbin Way? That I could see, but... Well, I digress. Sometimes there's just no rhyme or reason.

As she was walking around in the boat, I couldn't help but notice that the woman was more than six feet tall, having long shapely legs and wearing what looked like hot pants. I wondered why she had this aversion to not getting her feet wet. There was no argument, either. She was not going to get her feet wet, and it was her that came up with the solution.

Her: "Pull the nose of the boat so that it's almost inside the driver's side car door and I'll step from the front of the boat into the car without getting wet."

Him: "I hope nobody's watching."

Too late, my friend. Too late!

Carefully, he pulled the two-seat boat at an odd angle, and placed the nose of the boat as close as he could near the open SUV door where Princess Long Legs smoothly crossed from the boat into the driver's seat without touching the warm waters of Bauneg Beg Lake. He didn't look thrilled with the process. Now he was left alone to manage loading the boat.

Once Princess was safely and dryly in the SUV, he turned the boat toward open water and mounted the vessel and started it. I assumed he would do a quick turn in the cove and mount the waiting trailer. Once started, it seems he decided that another quick trip around the pond was warranted. Leaving the cove at high speed and creating a deep wake, he bounced three or four of the docked pontoon boats in the cove as he started down the lake, leaving the vehicle, the trailer, and his wife behind with no word of his return. Several minutes later, he returned to the ramp, mounted the trailer, and got off to attach the winch tow strap to the front of the boat. Once done, he cranked the boat up onto the dry trailer and *asked* the lady driver to pull ahead. Once on dry land, he got in the passenger's side of the SUV and they proceeded to leave the area. I'm not sure if it was the vodka, but it sure looked like Lady Long Legs was driving from the back seat! Yeah, it's the vodka.

STORY TWO

It was the middle day of a long holiday weekend and the weather was as perfect as one would want. Despite the great weather, the traffic on the lake was light and unusually quiet for such a perfect day. I was sitting on the deck in my new zero-gravity recliner reading the oceanic exploits of another Clive Cussler novel when I heard activity on the ramp. Yeah, it was my favorite time of year... when vacationers and renters go home. I felt like a Walmart greeter, "Take your boat and get out!"

A truck was slowly backing down the ramp to actually launch a 16-foot bow rider with a 60 hp outboard. *Hey*, I thought, *You're supposed to be taking boats out, not launching them.* As they approached the waterline at the shallow ramp, the two men got out of the truck and released the tie-down straps holding the boat to the trailer. One man climbed into the boat, and the other proceeded to the truck to get this show underway. And what a show it was, my friend. I was not disappointed. As many times as I've seen these *Keystone Kops* moments, I never get tired of them. One, they're too funny, and two, they're free.

Once the boat was untied and the guys were ready to launch, Boat Guy tells Truck Guy to back out into deep water, so the boat floats easily by itself. Wanting to oblige, Truck Guy began backing in at a slow pace, when all of a sudden the boat came screaming off the back end of the trailer, forcing the front end to suddenly point skyward, and drive the back end with the heavy motor down into the shallow ramp, crunching dirt and gravel and plowing backwards until the boat floated on its own. The boat was temporarily shrouded in a mushroom of dark, muddy water. Yeah, that propeller will have to be replaced.

If you haven't guessed by now, the trailer was equipped with bogey wheels instead of the more popular and safer carpeted wood bunks. The boat was actually riding on a pair of roller skates when it abruptly left the angled trailer, soaring into the shallow depths of the ramp.

Truck Guy stayed where he was in the water until Boat Guy started the boat, making sure it would actually start after trying to drive it backwards at an awkward angle into the bottom of the lake. It looked like a scene from the *Titanic* sinking for a brief moment. Sans Kate Winslet, of course.

As soon as the motor started, Boat Guy revved the engine enough to cause an oily blue haze, thus killing two local mosquito nests and wilting some nearby lake blossoms. After settling into a normal idle, he says: "Hey, there's water coming in here!"

Truck Guy: "Yeah, it might have been in there from before."

Before what?

Boat Guy: "I don't think so. It's coming in pretty fast. Stay right there. I think I need to reload the boat. Get the trailer out further if you can."

Truck Guy: "Okay." And he backs up enough to cover the bogey wheels... and stops.

Boat Guy: "Never mind, I got it. I found the plugs floating in the well and I stuffed them back in. I think the water stopped."

Truck Guy: "Go fast around the lake and take out a plug. The boat will drain from the back."

And with that, the boat left the cove at high speed and the truck returned to wherever it came from. Were they residents? Vacationers? Not sure. But watching them recreate the scene from a famous movie was fun. Not sure if these guys were smart enough to check for any damage to the motor or propeller.

Now, where was I in that novel? I really hope I'm home when they take the boat out.

STORY THREE

I was enjoying my morning coffee, overlooking the calm waters of the lake, reflecting on the wonderful, warm summer we were lucky to enjoy this year. The weather reminded me of the long, hot summers of my youth, playing baseball, going to the beach, nights at the drive-in theater, and visiting the local amusement parks with family and friends. Yeah, those were the good old days. I bet you remember those days too! These days, I can't remember what I had for breakfast or what I did yesterday. Taking a sip of java, I was broken out of my daydreaming by the chirping of my ever present cell phone. It was a local neighbor reaching out with news he thought I should know about. Since the Lake Mayor passed in 2019, it seems that I may have taken his place, or maybe the residents just seem to contact me for whatever... how the heck do I get roped into everything about the lake, anyway? According to the wife... I'm easy. Maybe so, honey. Maybe so.

Phone: "Hi Ron. I have a tree removal happening on my property near Corbin Way, and it will take a couple of hours. They will be blocking the road to remove a tree from my back yard."

Me: "You should be okay, but I'll let the area folks know, and I'll let Parker's know."

Phone: "I don't think I know them. What's their first names?"

He must be the only guy on the lake that doesn't know about Parker's Boathouse. The company enjoys some twenty-five customers on the lake and uses Corbin Way for twenty-three of them twice a year. Everyone knows Mark Parker. Well, maybe not.

Me: "It's the marina that has twenty-five customers here, and they use Corbin Way."

Phone: "Oh, I thought it was the house next to The Botanists."

So, I did what I do, notified people even though this was not my affair, so to speak. People just get me involved. I think it's because I usually get things done. I contacted Parker's Boathouse, the local neighbors, the Bauneg Beg Lake general membership through Facebook, and the lake website, letting folks know the ramp road would be closed for several hours for the tree removal work. I went the extra mile too, in contacting the Bauneg Beg Lake Mosquito Coalition, the Regional Office of Chipmunk Affairs, the National Aviary Consortium, and the area Chapter of Squirrels Local 4073. My work was done.

About an hour later, I heard a screeching woodchipper start up and begin chewing the fallen branches and tree limbs that had already been removed from the 95-foot rotting tree. The noise level was really high, even from my cottage more than 120 feet away. My tinnitus was on overload. Was it too early for vodka and Coke? (Does it matter?) And, they were, in fact, blocking Corbin Way as a safety precaution. After several minutes of the loud, ear-piercing grinding, I thought I'd walk to the end of my driveway to take a look at the operation first hand. As I approached the end of the driveway, I noticed an

SUV sitting in the middle of the road and assumed he was waiting to go by the work area.

On closer inspection, I found the SUV was part of the work site. The front windows were down and the occupant, which I couldn't see, had his radio playing some ungodly style of music I'd never heard before, at ear-piercing levels, all the while playing on his cell-phone. On the front of his vehicle there was a ¾ inch, 200-foot length of rope that extended from his tow hook under the front bumper up to the top of the tree, just above the climber's head. What?

I had arrived just in time to see the SUV back up a little, taking tension on the tree top and finally pulling it toward the road where they wanted it to land. The SUV pulled forward, and the climber yelled at him to stay where he was.

That didn't work. The way too loud music, the cell phone, the inattention... Yeah, that didn't go well. So the climber yelled down to worker Number 2 on the ground and told him to go tell SUV Guy to stay where he was for another section he needed to rope off and pull down. Worker #2 didn't really look too ambitious about talking to SUV Guy. But I noticed another worker as part of the four-person crew. SHE was a tall, gangly, short-haired woman trying hard to stay away from Worker #2 and SUV Guy. Maybe she was the grinder operator.

The climber readjusted himself some 15.65864 feet lower on the de-limbed tree to make another cut with his short-bladed chainsaw. Using a chase line, he brought the end of the long rope to his perch and tied it to the top of the next section to be cut. All of a sudden, and without being told, SUV Guy decided to back up and take a strain on the long rope, putting tension on the tree. That really irked climber guy.

Climber: "Hey, stop! Stop! The tree is rotted on the inside and it could break below me. Don't back up."

SUV Guy was busy listening to heavy metal music, playing on his cell phone, and couldn't hear a hand grenade if it went off next to him.

Climber: (to Worker # 2) "Go tell him not to back up until I tell him."

And so the instruction came to SUV Guy again to play nice. However, as the climber was cutting the next 10-foot section, and getting most of the way through, SUV Guy abruptly, and without being told, backed up and actually broke the ten-foot section before the cut was completed. That was pretty dangerous. Climber Guy wasn't happy and had the long rope disconnected and coiled. He'd had enough.

The workers did the rest of the cutting and grinding without the need for ropes or help from SUV Guy. This could have (should have) been SUV Guy's last job with the company. While the SUV had pulled over to the side of Corbin Way, the music was still blaring, and he never exited the vehicle. It all ended up without an OSHA site visit, and nobody getting hurt, but it could have been so much worse. The boat ramp road was opened again by mid-afternoon, no one having been impacted by the tree removal work.

This was not the typical ramp road story you've come to expect, but still you never know what's going to happen on the infamous boat ramp road called Corbin Way.

front yard /
back yard

T he fall season was just around the corner, and with that meant the residents, visitors, renters, and vagabonds were removing their boats, keeping the private way busy as the season was coming to a close. And what a season it had been. The area in southern Maine endured a near perfect summer with above average temperatures, below average rainfall, and no significant weather-related issues anyone could complain about. It's human nature to complain about something, but not about the weather this year. Yet it was coming to an end and the Dam Committee was getting ready to drop the water for the season. Thus, getting boats out of the water was on everyone's list of things to do... and soon.

The exodus started in early October and the ramp on Corbin Way was getting busier and busier. This is usually my location for watching the goings-on, knowing someone will put on a show for me. I hardly ever get disappointed. It's funny that many folks who use the ramp look over to the perch at my cottage to see if I'm there watching. Well, of course I am! Many ask, "Hey, will I be in one of your stories?" And I reply, "Only if you do something stupid." I think that response makes them focus on the task at hand.

FRONT YARD

I was reading a novel by my favorite author and the exploits of at sea adventures of conspiracy and worldwide mayhem. It was better than watching Hallmark Christmas movies with The First Mate. I never ever watched a Hallmark movie where I heard stuff like, "Avast, ye scurvy dog!" Or, "It'll be the yardarm for ye!" Or, "Ahoy, me matey!" Or "Avast, thar she blows!" Or, "How would you like my peg shoved up your Davy Jones Locker?" But I digress.

A black pickup truck was having a hard time keeping the trailer straight as he was approaching the ramp to pick up an 18-foot bow rider floating calmly offshore. After several tries, he was finally able to get the truck and trailer in position in the shallow ramp to trailer his boat with the lady at the helm. Once the trailer was in the water, he got out of the truck (the water was pretty cold) and went to the trailer winch to unravel the heavy duty nylon strap. In the meantime, the helmswoman was intent on her cellphone, not even noticing her husband was turning three shades of blue with cold water up to his thighs. Trying to get her attention didn't work at first, since he had other issues to deal with.

Not wanting to get his pants wet, he hiked his shorts up into a nice wedgie. So much so that he looked like he was wearing a thong at a pool party. And so far, the helmswoman still wasn't aware her ride had arrived. I wondered how long this was going to go on. So, while she played some game on her phone, he decided to release the winch clutch and yank out the heavy strap the full length of the trailer. In doing so, the metal handle was slapping the water at high revolutions as he pulled the strap out manually. All the time, he was spraying water on himself from head to waterline. He didn't look like he was having a great time. And the wife? Yeah, still unaware. I could see the motor running, but she was still just sitting there waiting.

What seemed like forever, she finally looked up and saw the trailer and the blue man standing in thigh high water, wearing a wet thong she didn't remember him bringing. Slowly, like really slowly, she approached the trailer and shut off the motor. From there, Blue

Man muscled the boat in position, attaching the strap from the winch to the boat's bow cleat. Walking back to the winch crank, and pulling up his wet pants-thong, he ably brought to boat up on the trailer. Once on, he got in the truck and pulled the rig out of the water. Yeah, she was still on her cellphone. Maybe I should have offered the guy a drink. I mean, who wears thongs in October?

The following day, there was more mischief on the ramp. Looking out over the front of the cottage, some commotion on the ramp caught my eye. There was a 15-foot aluminum bass boat with an outboard motor being tied up to some shrubs near the ramp. The male occupant got out of the boat, removed a two-wheeled bicycle, and promptly rode up Corbin Way to parts unknown. At the same time, two of my neighbors came cruising into Patriot Cove with their pontoon boats. I soon found out that a local marina was on the way with two trucks and trailers to remove their vessels. It would be hard to do with a fishing boat at the ramp and bike boy gone. So, I did what any good neighbor would do... got involved. Yeah, yeah, I know. I hear that from the wife all the time.

I walked over to the ramp and found the aluminum craft blocking the entire area, blown there by the stiff breeze. I untied the rope and pulled the boat to the opposite side of the ramp where it would be out of the way of the two trailers that were soon coming. Where was this guy and when was he coming back? I didn't have to wait long before he showed up with his SUV and a trailer. Backing down the right-of-way is no easy task for the unlearned. Try as he might, he kept jackknifing the trailer over and over again. When he was still 120.8680 feet from the ramp, I decided to walk up the road and manually lift the light trailer, placing it in the center of the road hoping he would eventually get it in the water. We finally hit pay dirt after several more minutes. Getting out of the SUV, he noticed the two pontoons out in the bay. "Looks like a busy day out here."

I mentioned that more trailers were coming soon, and he needed to be out of the way. Obliging, he quickly got the boat on the trailer and was soon on his way to wherever he came from. Seeing he peddled a bike, it had to be somewhere close. You have to ask yourself, though. He had out-of-state vehicle plates, no boat registration sticker, no required milfoil sticker, and he was trespassing on the ramp. How could he know the ramp was even here? No wonder I talk to myself.... And yes, the two pontoons were soon removed by the marina folks and all our lives returned to normal. Well, until the next time. The next two weeks would be very busy on Corbin Way! I had some vodka and Coke, a sharp pencil, and my 1943 BUPERS, Busch and Lomb 7 x 50 Navy Bridge Binoculars. Bring it!

BACK YARD

Several days later, I began to clean up the backyard of the early fallen leaves, pine needles, some pinecones, and other debris the trees were shedding. Even at this early stage, I had a truck full of stuff to go to the dump. While working out near the road, two of my neighbors came by getting their afternoon exercise in.

The first neighbor was a man pushing a carriage with his baby daughter in it, and his dog tethered to the side. I stopped raking, thinking I was about to engage in conversation with him. It was a good day to get to know your neighbors better. As he approached, he took out his cellphone as if in concentrated conversation and passed me by with no acknowledgement that I was even there. I stared at him, but he kept his head down and hustled by, not wanting to be engaged. Okay, then! I wonder if his dog would have been friendlier. Maybe next time.

Not ten minutes later, I saw a young lady walking her dog my way. When she saw me near the road, she crossed to the far side and immediately got on her cell phone and passed by without hesitation. What was going on? I had my false tooth in, so it's not like I looked like the neighborhood child molester. I took a shower the night before. I even had my Navy Veteran ball cap on. That always solicits kind remarks and acknowledgements from people. Even at Walmart. Yet, right here in my own back yard I couldn't even muster a hello.

Maybe it was a sign of the times. People are constantly buried in the cellphones and human interaction is nearly a thing of the past.

Not for everyone, but for some. Reminds me of a cartoon I saw recently that is relevant.

A man enters heaven and complains to St. Peter that his life had something missing. St. Peter says, "Well, you started off right, but you buried yourself in your cell phone and missed everything." Isn't that true? I still have two neighbors I don't know and maybe never will. But, my yard is clean!

the neighbor

T rying to live the quiet life on a lake is not always how things work out. For me, I was somewhat fortunate to live on a quiet tree-lined lane off of a busy county road in southern Maine. For the most part, life was quiet, simple, and as busy as you wanted it to be. I also had the good fortune of living next to some good neighbors. And while old Edgar was a quiet neighbor, he was also a recluse. He didn't want to be bothered, helped, or given advice unless he asked for it. And that was nearly never. Edgar was his own man. He was seen as a beer-drinking, grouchy curmudgeon who kept to himself and expected you to do the same.

Edgar had a boat tied to his dock aptly called *The Plum*. That's because that was exactly the color of the 16-foot bow rider that was of the 1980s vintage. It sported an outboard motor that had to be at least twenty-five years old. He used the boat now and then to cruise the lake in the late afternoon, taking a can or two of his favorite brew to enjoy along his journey. Usually, within an hour, he could be seen and heard coasting back into his dock. Some days, he was seen sitting in the front bow area, paddling his way back in.

While sitting on my front deck, reading a novel of my favorite author and enjoying a cold beverage on a warm day, I saw Edgar come paddling around the corner of Windy Way Point, still 300 yards from his dock. Did I mention Edgar was in his 80s? I was taken by the site of an 80-year-old man working so hard paddling water trying to get home. So I did what any good neighbor would do.

Me: "Hey Edgar, do you want me to come out there and tow you to your dock?"

Edgar: "No!"

Me: "Are you sure? I'm not busy."

Edgar: "No, thanks!"

I know when my services aren't needed. So I returned to my perch and watched Edgar work his way back to his dock some three houses over. He looked pretty tired to me. Minutes after he docked, I saw him outside with a cold beer sitting at his metal picnic table. He seemed to enjoy the solitude and being lost in his own thoughts.

The next afternoon, Edgar again took *The Plum* out for a tour of the lake, this time breaking down in the center of Patriot Cove. Trying to restart the engine several times, and only until the battery died, did he break out the trusty oar and begin paddling his way back to shore. I was not going to ask him again if he needed my help.

One day, soon after, I noticed some commotion around his dock. There were three men sporting the same T-shirts advertising some local marina. They were in Edgar's boat, busily removing the older broken outboard. I had so many questions. Why was the boat still in the water and not onshore for this work? I forgot the other questions. Once they had the old broken motor out of the way, they brought down a new 75 hp outboard motor. It was black, shiny, but looked out of place on the older plum-colored boat that had seen its better years. Edgar had too, but he was still living the life... as cranky as he was.

A couple of hours later, the work was done. The marina technicians started the new motor and took the boat around the cove for a spin to check things out, making certain all the linkages, electronics, and engine performance were working properly. After a few minutes, the crew returned to the dock, assuring Edgar his new ride was ready for the rest of the summer and beyond. He quickly dismissed them, as I heard him say, "Okay, thanks a lot." Edgar was a man of brevity.

They left the old motor propped up against his house where he wanted it. It was 400 pounds of useless junk they offered to get rid of. But it was Edgar's property, and he was going to hold on to it.

That same afternoon, after the crew left the property, Edgar climbed into the boat and started the engine. It came to life and purred like the 400 pound engine it was. It sounded powerful and ready for a ride down the lake. After sitting there letting the boat idle for what seemed like forever, he finally threw off the dock lines and headed out into the cove for his maiden voyage.

About forty-five minutes had gone by when, from my perch, I saw Edgar come around the corner of Windy Way Point. While I would have expected him to be cruising at any speed, he was again sitting on the bow of the boat, paddling his way back to his dock. Really? Maybe he should rename the boat *The Lemon*! Forgetting my last offer, I called out again.

Me: "Edgar, do you want me to come out and tow you to your dock?"

Edgar: "No!"

Some fifteen minutes later, he was pulling into his dock, noticeably exhausted. This had to be a lot of exertion for an eighty-year-old cranky man. Plus, he had to be upset that he had just spent $7,000 on a brand new motor and now he was paddling his way home from who knows how far out on the lake. I felt bad for the old man. New motor, same day, and an immediate breakdown. Like it was his nature, he went into the house, got a beer, and came out to sit at his metal picnic table wondering what to do.

Soon after his time of contemplation, he got up, went into his garage, and came out with a screwdriver. He removed the motor's cover and began fiddling around with all sorts of screw adjustments, from linkage to fuel, and idle, to whatever screw he could turn. Yeah, this wasn't going to end well. And it didn't. From that day on, he would start the motor and it would just sit there and billow stinky dark blue heavy oil-laden smoke that rolled out over the waters of Patriot Cove, causing what one would think was an eclipse of the sun. The boat never left the dock again. Ever. But... we're not done here.

Maybe it was out of spite, anger, old age or whatever, but *every day*, seven days a week, old Edgar would walk out to the dock, start the engine and let it spew the heavy, gaseous and oily smoke that drifted out into the Cove. You could set your clock at 4:50 p.m. every single day... unless it was raining. While the motor roughly idled and spewed its mosquito-killing venom, old Edgar would mount his John Deere ride-on lawn mower with the 36-inch cutting deck and drive around his house, cutting all the grass he could find. Every day at 4:50 pm. Every day!

When he finished cutting whatever blades of grass he could find, he would then, and only then, shut off the boat motor and allow the blue haze covering the cove to slowly evaporate.

Edgar had two cats and both of them were hunters. Whenever they captured any game, they would proudly bring it to Edgar so they could celebrate (I guess). Whenever Edgar would cut his grass on The Mayor's side of the house, the mower would grind up the little critters (mice, chipmunks, moles, birds) and splatter the remains on the side of The Mayor's truck. The Mayor mentioned this gross injustice to Edgar, but it fell on deaf ears. The murdering mower continued on a regular basis. Each day, the truck looked like a murder scene, with blood splatter as proof. The Mayor had little choice but to go to the local car wash several times a week. The Mayor was a very tolerant man.

By the next summer, the boat and motor remained idle, and The Mayor stopped doing daily car wash visits. Edgar? Well, he just sat at his metal picnic table refusing help, slugging down beer and eating store-bought pizza.

Life is good on the lake. A little more than quirky at times, but I wouldn't trade lake life for anything. Maybe one day in the future, any one of us could become Edgar. Maybe I should start looking for a round metal picnic table.

that will leave a mark

The First Mate and I had just finished tying down the outside deck furniture and were ready to call it a day, thinking we provided sufficient protection from the coming winds and heavy snow until next spring. In the past week, the ramp along Corbin Way had been a beehive of activity, with folks anxious to remove their boats before the water was lowered in the days ahead. Nobody wanted to come to camp and find their boats sitting in the mud or rocks where there was normally sufficient water for their activities. I knew the upcoming weekend was sure to be very busy and the dam committee was opening the dam on Thursday. Within three days, the ramp would be useless to anyone but kayakers and canoeists.

After returning my tools to the shed, I could hear a faint alarm in the distant. I asked the wife who also thought it was some type of alarm, but couldn't be sure as we had never heard that particular sound before. It could have been a car alarm in the distance, or a fire or smoke alarm with weak batteries. Looking further, some rustling through the trees up the street gave up the mysterious alarm. It was a black pickup truck trying to back a long pontoon trailer onto Corbin

Way... with some difficulty. Okay... *lots* of difficulty. But he had an alarm!

His first attempt ended up in a jackknife situation that made him pull up and out of the ramp road onto the main road. The second try was slow and painful and ended up in another jackknifing. *How long was this going to take? I wondered. And if another resident or marina's truck showed up to pick up a boat, how would this situation work out?*

So, for the second time in ten minutes, the driver pulled back onto the main road, but further up the street, I supposed, to get a better angle at backing into the right of way. And again, he jackknifed the trailer and had to pull out again. Yep, this was getting painful to watch. And yet, why was I enjoying it so? It was time for a cold beverage of which I had an ample closet of choice libations. In the meantime, the pontoon boat was patiently circling the cove, waiting... and waiting.

On his next attempt, there was trespassing involved. Backing the long 20-foot trailer, he misjudged the Corbin Way entry and turned (actually jackknifed again) into a resident's driveway located just a couple of feet from the ramp road entry. He soon found the scenery was a lot different. That dog was really upset at seeing a long steel trailer coming into his domain. The error was soon noticed, of course, and he was pulling back onto the main road for the umpteenth time. I wondered what he was thinking. Maybe I should go out there and help the guy. Yeah, maybe I... no... no.

It took another few times before he was able to get the trailer down the road and slowly; I mean painstakingly slowly, backed the trailer down the road toward the waiting pontoon. After what seemed like forever, he finally made it to the water's edge and slowly backed the trailer into the shallow ramp and buried the trailer bunks under-water... right where he needed to be. Finally.

Now it was time to see if they could actually trailer the boat. I always love this part. There are always variables that come into play that sometimes, I mean most times, people don't take into considera-tion. Is it windy? Is your motor trimmed up properly? Are you using your cell phone's GPS to find the sunken trailer? Do you even know the trailer was waiting for you? How fast should you approach the trailer? Yeah, it's a pretty technical evolution not to be taken lightly.

Once the trailer was somewhere underwater, the lady helmsperson made her first approach to the unseen carrier with only the front winch posts showing above water. Not taking into account the northerly stiff breeze, she instantly floated sideways, missing the trailer completely. Great start! She backed out into the cove for another try. Same thing happened as she neared her objective and had to back out again and retry. And then again for a third time. Watching from my perch, I noticed that the lady captain was putting the outboard motor in neutral long before she attempted to mount the trailer. That never works. Any decent seaman knows that when you give up steerage, the vessel will float in whatever direction you last had it, or the wind will take you off course instantly. Such was this case. Finally, on her umpteenth approach (see, they have something in common), the large platform boat made it over the sunken rails, and she was instructed to power the boat the rest of the way forward. That put an end to the endless drifting, anyway.

Now, stopped within 10 feet of the trailer winch and having the boat 70.39485% loaded, The First Mate, who was patiently waiting in the cold water of the ramp, started to unwind the heavy nylon winch strap. He unraveled what seemed like 15 feet. He slowly made his way across the trailer's frame to attach the strap to the front center bow cleat. Then, walking back to the winch, he began to crank in the excess strapping before finally pulling it taut. With way too much effort, he cranked the winch until his arms hurt. Maybe the trailer wasn't that far underwater. Finally, the boat reached the winch and settled on the trailer's bunks. The lady captain sat quietly, amusing herself on her cell phone.

After announcing he was done and ready to drive the truck out, she asked, "Can I get off the boat now?" He replied, "Why don't you wait until I get you on dry land so you don't get wet." What the heck was she thinking? So, accepting her fate, she sat down and resumed her cell phone games.

He slowly drove the rig out of the water and started to pull up the road some, when some low-lying tree branches caught the nice lady, unaware, in the head, sending her long follicles flying backwards, hither to and fro, and causing her to drop her prized cell phone on the deck. Her hair looked like she'd stuck a finger in an electrical outlet. She felt her face where the branch hit her... yeah, that will leave a mark. The driver... never saw it happen.

It would have been nice to hear their conversation on the way home. Hey, it's just another day on the ramp.

So, looking forward to tomorrow.

winter woes

It was an unusual winter in Maine. In past years, New England, and Maine in particular, would be the unfortunate recipient of heavy doses of freezing rain, snow measured in feet, and high winds. These mostly Canadian borne storms would start pounding the state by late November or early December, dragging out the long winters through late March into April. Yeah, I believe in climate change, especially here on the shores of the lake. In the thirty years I've lived on the shores of Bauneg Beg Lake, the ice out date each year has never been later than April 15th. And in only two of those years had the lake defrosted completely, first by March 15th and last year ice out was declared on March 7th. A new record.

We were now in the third week of January, and where there was typically a foot or two of snow, there were instead dried frozen lawns, dirty looking landscapes, a frozen pond, and fairly mild weather. I wondered when it would all come crashing down around us. It had to arrive at some point. This was Maine, after all.

Going into the third week of January, the local meteorologists, with their super Doppler 4000 and other up-to-date modern weather predictions like Punxsutawney Phil, the Japanese Spy Satellite hovering over the USA, or some unknown weather station in Guam, started predicting what would be our first plowable snowstorm. I was giddy with excitement. Finally, some roof insulation to capture the heat I was losing and paying for through the roof (pun intended).

As was my modus operandi, I got ready for the projected 4 to 8-inch storm that would blanket the area with snow, giving us a beautiful white landscape. I was ready. On the heels of the storm would be a massive Arctic Blast that would send the temperatures plummeting well below zero. In preparation, I got out my three manly shovels, put my trash barrels inside the gambrel shed, made sure the snow blower was operating, had my roof rake ready, and extra gas in a five-gallon can. I was ready!

The night the storm rolled in, I had gone to bed early in anticipation of the coming morning and the sight of the newly fallen, light and fluffy snow. Despite being retired and not having a lot to do this time of year, I was up before daybreak and dressed for snow removal. What the heck was wrong with me? I had all day, and yet, I wanted to get out there and blow rooster tails of snow 80 feet in any direction. I was as giddy as a 10-year-old on Christmas morning.

After a light breakfast, I stuck my feet in my warm 30-year-old boots and started out for the shed. I was ready to meet the day.

As I normally did, I went to get my Ariens, 21-inch, 4-stroke snowblower, out of the shed. It was gassed up, pointing in the right direction and ready to go. I put the key in the door padlock only to find the lock was frozen. Before the snow arrived during the night, we had some freezing rain that got into the Master lock and froze it up. I have zero patience, so I was miffed right at the start. I went into the house to get a plastic candle lighter, you know, like a long plastic and metal Zippo lighter. The thing worked great in the house, but when I got it outside, it refused to work. That piece of crap! I wanted to stomp on it and crush it to smithereens. I doubt the wife would have appreciated that though, so I thought better of it and calmed myself down a little. I returned the lighter back to the house and went back out to the shed. Now what? I couldn't do any snow removal as all the gear was behind the door with the frozen lock.

Then an idea struck me. I went to the cellar and retrieved my small propane tank and screwed on the self-starting propane igniter. That certainly would produce enough heat to warm the lock and melt the ice holding it captive. Proud to have thought of this easy fix, I quickly returned to the shed with my blow torch in hand. Once there, I opened the gas nozzle on the starter, and pressed the small red ignition button to set off a flame a satellite could see. I was again disappointed. The tank had run out of propane almost immediately and refused to light the torch. Okay, this isn't funny!

I knew I had a second propane tank in the cellar and went back to retrieve it. I tried it before I took it with me, making certain it worked. It had produced a 2-inch long blue flame that would certainly do the trick. With my new ice weapon in hand, I returned to the shed's frozen lock. This time, the flame burned bright. Within thirty seconds, the ice melted, and the lock opened easily, bringing a smile to my face.

First, I grabbed my 17-foot roof rake so I could remove the snow build up on the wife's portable garage. Walking around the structure and finding a good starting point, I raised the rake to the peak, only to find the rake was broken. It had lost a nut and bolt holding one side of the plastic rake to the metal frame, making it not only wobbly, but now capable of possibly tearing a hole in the heavy canvas cover. So, facing another delay, I went to the workshop and finally found the right size nut and bolt to replace the lost ones. After several minutes of repair and straightening the rake, I was again ready to resume the work. What else could go wrong? And why is my inner child laughing? (We don't have a great relationship.)

After cleaning the portable garage and the truck carport roofs, I noticed a large snow pile hanging out over the house's entrance door. I walked over to remove it with my newly repaired roof rake when a gust of wind came up and blew the pile of snow off the edge, hitting me square in the face and chest, getting snow inside my jacket, covering my face, and instantly fogging my glasses. I started speaking in tongues, not knowing anything I was saying. My irritation was getting out of control. And my driveway was still full of untouched snow. This was not my typical day. And I was so looking forward to a fun day! So far, not so much!

I cleaned myself up and got my glasses back in place, ready to go again. It was time to get the snowblower out there and do some major snow removal. I turned on the required gas valve, set the choke, turned on the key, and primed the starter. I yanked on the pull cord. Usually it started on the second pull, every time, every year. Today, no freaking way! I wanted to take a 5-pound ball peen hammer and give it something NOT to start for. What the heck was happening?

I went to the workshop again and got an extension cord I could use to start the machine electrically. I returned to the other side of the shed, hooked up the cord to an outlet, and hit the electric starter button on the side of the piece of junk I used to blow snow. After several moments of sputtering, coughing, and grinding (no... not me), the machine started belching blue smoke, but kicked into high gear, eventually running normally. I removed the cord and was ready to go. As I made my way outside and down the small wooden ramp, the machine stalled. I wanted to scream. After a quick check, I had run out of gas. That was easily taken care of, and soon I was back to work.

From that point, I was able to work trouble free, clearing the entire driveway area and the roadside area around the mailboxes. Things were looking up. Luckily for me, my lovely bride had taken the time to clean the front main deck and the stairs for me. That was a pleasant surprise and made me happy to cut my work short after a difficult start.

Completing the work, I returned the snow blower to the shed, cleaned it of the excess snow, gassed it up for the next time, and called it a day.

Considering the frozen lock, an empty propane fuel tank, a broken roof rake, getting slapped with a falling snowbank, and a snow blower that refused to start and then running out of gas... it wasn't the fun day I had envisioned. But hey, my patience held on, and I still have a candle lighter!

Anyone want a slightly used but sarcastic inner child? Free!

Living the Life on Bauneg Beg Lake series

Turn the page for free short stories!

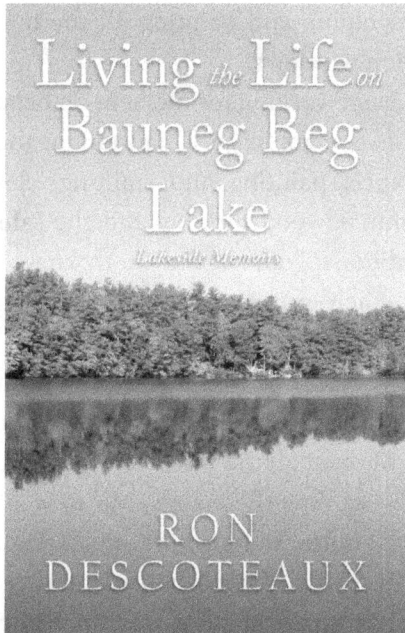

A FREE short story from
Living the Life on Bauneg Beg Lake
Lakeside Memoirs

ME, MARIO, AND THE PAINT JOB

It was in the summer of 2012 that our neighbors on the point, Bob and Sue, had hired our two teenage grandsons to do some needed maintenance on their cottage and property. The boys had worked very hard during their April school vacation to rake out the entire property, remove brush and tree limbs that had fallen during the hard winter storms, and had returned the grounds around their lake cottage to the pristine condition that one would expect whenever you visited the cottage at the end of Corbin Way. The owners were so happy with the quality of the work that they asked Mario and Niklas if they would consider doing more work for them. The boys were being tasked with cleaning and flushing the roof gutters, cleaning and staining the large rear wooden deck and stairs, painting the garage door, and scraping and painting all the house windows and casement foundation windows.

The boys had been working for me here on beautiful Bauneg Beg Lake for the past five years or so. I had taught them to do routine grounds maintenance, painting and staining, cleaning the boats, insulation work, minor woodworking, and the safe use and care of powered and hand tools. Point is, they both knew their way around this type of work. Each grandson had his own way of doing work. Once in a while, one aggravates the other.

This particular project involved Mario, who was relegated to paint the house windows. I asked the owner, Bob, to get two gallons of white house paint to cover all the work he wanted done. I knew I'd be spending quite a bit of time there since Mario would be working off tall ladders and I did not want him working up that high unattended. Plus, he likes to drop stuff. After I helped him clean and flush the gutters and paint the garage door, it was time to get to the serious work of painting the house windows.

I helped Mario tape out both sides of the windows (vision panels) on the garage doors and casement windows, and left him to complete his tasks. He didn't need me when he was working at ground level. Not that he ever asked for help, anyway. Every hour or so, I would leave the quiet of my estate and go find Mario to see how he was coming along. I knew Mario was not a fast worker, but God bless him, he was thorough.

When it came to working the windows off a ladder, I went to help him. I checked the paint level in his can and wondered why he had so much paint left. He had painted both sides of the garage door and the two casement windows, and the frame around the side entrance door. Yet the paint can looked nearly full. I checked the work he had already done, and it looked fine. I guess it was just me.

I set up the ladder for him to work the high windows myself, ensuring the ladder's feet were firmly planted on the uneven ground and the ladder was safe from moving side to side. Let me tell you about the painting of one typical window, and you can just imagine what the rest of the project went like.

It was about 11 a.m. and Mario was perched high up the ladder, scraping off any loose paint and removing debris like pine needles, small twigs stuck in the siding around the window frame, and swiping away any minor leavings with a rag. After several minutes, he was ready for the paint can and brush, ready to tackle the window. My job was to stay at the bottom of the ladder to keep it steady, pick up anything he would drop (and he would), and keep him company while regaling him with stories of my youth. It was a warm, breeze-less day, just right for painting... and storytelling! Mario was a pretty quiet kid, so I kind of talked to myself most of the time, getting a well-timed grunt from him now and then.

I had rigged a plastic bucket (plastic coffee container) with a wire loop that he could use to hang the paint bucket on a ladder rung, thus keeping his hands free to work. When he was finally ready, he started on the window. By now, we're twelve minutes into this window and he has not dipped his brush yet.

He started by dipping his brush into the bucket, and like he was taught, slipping the sides of the brush against the sides of the bucket, removing excess paint to avoid dripping when reaching for the window pane. He wiped the brush so many times, I wondered if he left any paint of the bristles. I knew he didn't have enough paint on his brush to make a stain, yet he spread that drop (maybe two) over a two-foot area of the window's frame. He brushed it on, back and forth, back and forth, back and... well, you get it right? Then he does it all over again, dip, swipe, swipe, swipe, and spread another two drops against the window frame, back and forth, back and forth... and did this painstakingly until the whole window frame was done. I encouraged him to take at least *three* drops of paint, but it seemed he had his own method. It took forever to complete. I was looking for a cyanide capsule.

During the hour that it took to do this window, several side events happened to enhance my watching pleasure. About now, I'm talking to myself, in tongues no less.

I don't know how he did it, but while painting, he dropped his brush into the mulch and the bushes under the ladder. I had to retrieve the brush, clean it of the debris it had gathered, and get it back up to him. During the drop, the brush hit a rung or two, splattering paint drops over a wide area of the bush's small green leaves. The flowery bushes were between the house and the legs of the ladder, making a great target. Well, he dropped the brush a couple of times, getting more paint on the bushes than the windows. I said nothing.

At one point, while he was on the ladder, spreading out another two drops of paint, a jet ski came up the lake behind him, getting his attention. The whine of the machine at high speed, and the obvious enjoyment of its two occupants, was more than Mario could neglect. He stopped painting, turned his upper body almost 180 degrees (reminding me of Linda Blair, turning her head 360 degrees in the movie *The Exorcist*), and watched the machine race by. He must have had a better view than I did, because he was not returning to his work. After what seemed like forever, I banged on the ladder rung saying, "Hey, what are you doing?" To which he responded, "I couldn't help it."

He continued painting that window to completion. From start to finish, it took more than thirty-five minutes. For you and me, any more than ten minutes would have been really milking the project. So, you think he's ready to come down? Oh no. Not yet. "Pepere," he says. "Pass me the razor blade so I can clean the windows. There's a lot of pine sap and other stuff stuck on the glass." *Well*, I thought, *that's energetic of him*. I passed him the scraper and then spent another ten minutes watching him painstakingly scrape, scrape, and scrape an area not more than three square feet. My speaking in tongues had returned. I wondered what I was saying.

Finally coming off the ladder, he noticed the small paint drips on the bushes' leaves. He started taking each painted leaf off the bush (like he was picking blueberries) until there was no sign of the foreign paint on them. I can't even tell you how long that took. I looked into the paint bucket to see how much he would need for the next window, and the darn bucket was still full. This kid is good. He reminded me of Jesus with the fish and loaves. He was doing the same thing with paint. He was going to a Catholic College, it made sense. And to think, that was just the *first* window. We had a gazillion to go.

Now, just the opposite was true of his brother Niklas. Nik has spent many hours painting and staining, and had worn half the paint or stain as his trophies of his summer work. He lets the paint wash off as he showers during the week. He doesn't take it off with thinner or anything. He would have used both gallons of paint had he done the window project. Don't get me wrong, Nik does a great job. He just likes to show folks what he's been up to.

When Mario finished all the work, several days later, the owner could have saved a ton of money by getting a quart of paint and not two gallons. Yes, I stayed with Mario until the project was done. And yes, even today, I still speak in tongues. I wonder what I'm saying?

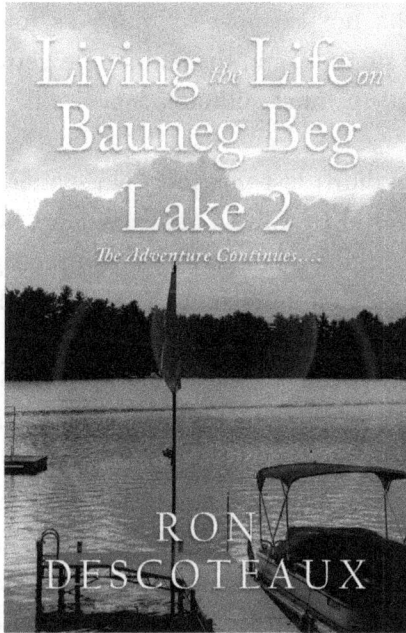

A FREE short story from
Living the Life on Bauneg Beg Lake 2
The Adventure Continues...

MULLETS AND MOTORS

I always looked forward with great anticipation to the onset of spring along the shores of beautiful Bauneg Beg Lake. The hard winter season had finally passed for another year, the warmer air trying to filter into New England, and the sights and sounds of the lake were coming to life. The loons arrived very early this year, serenading us with their haunting cry and eating 800 pounds of fish each year that I would never catch. Boat docks were in place wherever I looked, and many boats were already attached to their mooring systems. Ah, the life on Bauneg Beg Lake!

Enjoying my morning cup of joe, I was listening to the melodious sounds of lawnmowers, tractors, and a woodchipper doing their day's work. Okay, maybe not *enjoying* so much as tolerating. All of a sudden, the noise stopped, and the sudden peacefulness of the little cottage was bathed in quiet solitude. Maybe I'll have another cup of joe.

The tranquility didn't last that long. No sooner did I sit down to read my favorite novel by Clive Cussler, when I heard the familiar sound of a truck backing a boat trailer down the right of way to the boat launch. There's something about a rattling trailer backing down a dusty road that I knew would bring me the enjoyment I've come to know and love. The black pickup truck backed to the edge of the water and awaited its cargo. Me, I poured a vodka and Coke I knew I would need. (Something just told me I was about to be entertained.)

A few minutes passed when I first heard a high-pitched motor rounding the corner of Windy Way Point, home of the Royal Tier Garden and Butterfly Center. The boat looked like something out of the 60s or 70s. The driver did too! I checked my vodka and Coke, and being half full, I knew my eyes were not playing tricks on me. I had to check my drink, because I have a cataract in my left eye, and often-times, my inner child likes to play games with my vision. (Yeah, we still don't get along that great. She's very high-strung and opin-ionated!)

The approaching vessel was sitting low in the water and had the configuration of a typical fishing boat of the 70s. The noisy engine was older too, with a high rising engine cover that seemed to tower over the back of the transom. I had never seen the boat or the two men here before. I certainly would remember such a memorable ensemble. While I was taken back by the boat and older motor spewing oily smoke and making way too much noise, I was awed by the operator. He looked to be in his thirties, sporting a mullet and.... what I thought was a dark t-shirt, was a chest full of tattoos. Could have been my cataract, but I think it was tattoos. The noisy motor had been trimmed up way too far, and the propeller was barely in the water, making way too much noise and very little headway. Mullet (as I will refer to the operator) was racing the engine in hopes of keeping control of the boat. Then the engine stalled. He started the motor again, revving the smoky motor to the hilt, only to have it die out yet again. Maybe I would need another drink and earmuffs!

Seeing the boat and driver come around the corner of the point, I was surprised to see that the truck driver backed the trailer in far enough for an easy on load. That was refreshing all by itself. Usually, the driver doesn't want to get his tires wet, or get his exhaust pipe near the water, or thinks as long as the trailer is anywhere near the water, that should be enough, or in some cases, just doesn't care. Not this guy... he was out there. (Probably not as *far out* as his buddy!) So, he waited for Mullet to approach.

Mullet was still revving up the engine at top throttle with the propeller barely grazing the water. The engine turned over 8,000 rpm on the start and barely moved, since there was no traction in the water. Every time Mullet aimed the boat's bow toward the trailer, he would rev the engine, only to coast sideways. Then the engine would die. Mullet started the boat again with the usual high rev, causing an oily smoke cloud, only to drift from the trailer and try again. On a couple of attempts, the bow pointed toward the middle of the lake... really Mullet guy?

Driver Guy decided to help. With the truck (with a cap cover) in the water, he climbed onto the truck's wheel well, grabbing the top of the cover, and swinging himself over to the trailer tow bar. It was a nice acrobatic feat, I must say, then waited for the next attempt to trailer the boat. In the meantime, Mullet was still restarting the engine to a high-pitched rev, and the propeller still riding on top of the water. What was he not getting here? On the next attempt, he actually got the nose of the boat between the trailer bunks. This gave him confidence, it seemed, as he revved the engine so hard it stalled... and floated backwards... again. Time for another drink, I guess.

On my return, Driver Guy noticed me on the front deck, sitting there observing how the *Keystone Kops* load a boat. He shouted over to me, "It's his first time!" I yelled back, "Does his family let him procreate?" "What?" he asked. I replied, "Tell him to put the motor in the water so he can control the boat, or he'll be doing this all afternoon." The driver shouts to Mullet, "Put the motor in the water so you can control it and get the boat on the trailer!" Mullet replies, "Yeah... no!" And again the stalling of the motor and the drifting on a high rev continued. What was wrong with this guy?

After several (yes... several) more aimless attempts to trailer the boat, Mullet luckily sets the boat's bow between the trailer bunks. Now the starting and revving dance began at full tilt. The dance was on. I could barely see through the smoke. Time for yet another hit of vodka. Heck, if he was here any longer, I'd have to go to the store to reload the liquor cabinet.

After some continued high revving, the motor stalled one more time. Mullet thought he had enough grip on the trailer that he could manage to get it loaded from this position. So with 81.8578% of the boat out on the water (yet the propeller was hardly wet), Mullet walked to the front of the boat and gingerly stepped over the bow onto the trailer's front bar. No longer in the boat, he straddled the winch mechanism to loosen the strap. I'm thinking, *If this guy slips and falls off the trailer and lands crotch first on top of that tow bar, will I still be able to breathe through my uncontrollable laughter? Will he hear me, or will his pain be too excruciating? Will my wife make me go out and help him?*

Luckily (I suppose), he didn't fall off the trailer. So he lived to fight another day. It took several minutes for Mullet to unravel the tow strap, but finally got it hooked to the boat's bow cleat. He wasn't done his workout just yet. With the boat at least now tied to the winch, he moved to reel the boat in. With the large top heavy engine hanging off the back, it took Mullet several hard minutes on the winch to get the boat trailered enough for the next session. Now 80.675% on the trailer, the driver decided to drive the boat onto the right of way and complete the loading job from there. Yep... that always works!

Mullet saw me sipping my drink and yelled over, "It's my first time. Pretty good huh?" What could I say? For once, I had no words, so I continued sipping my beverage, trying to quiet my inner child. Then I watched them dry haul the boat the last six feet onto the trailer. Yeah... their first time, for sure.

Finally, the show was over, and I could return to the peace and tranquility of the lake I so loved and enjoyed. It was just a matter of time before the next show began. Heck, it wasn't even Memorial Day yet.

I guess I should go to the store. You never knew how long the next show might be.

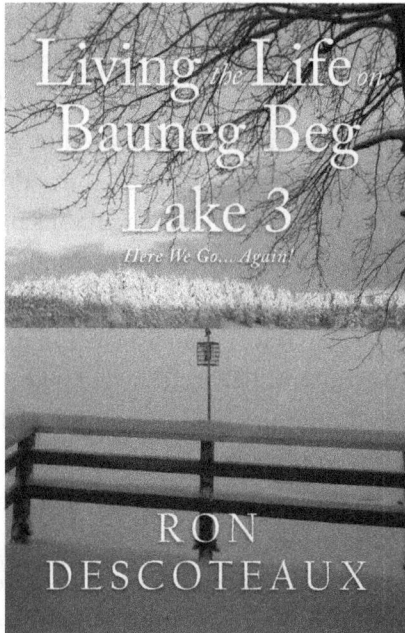

A FREE short story from
Living the Life on Bauneg Beg Lake 3
The Adventure Continues...

TIDBITS - FOUR SHORT STORIES

ONE: THE BOUNCER

Several years ago, when I thought I was invincible, I had purchased a 13-foot diameter, two ladder, two and a half foot thick (inflated) lake Bouncer (water trampoline) that the grandkids and I could enjoy while frolicking in the warm waters of beautiful Bauneg Beg Lake. It was a proud day when it arrived at the cottage on Javica Lane. I was happy that the grandsons were here to enjoy the long awaited, much anticipated delivery of the floating fun island we would enjoy together.

We unpacked the heavy box and quickly set out to inflate the gigantic tube and get it in the water so the fun could begin. Once inflated, we attached the rope and plastic rung boarding ladders on opposite sides of the large tube, and then proceeded with the anchor system. The ladder system had arrived, placed in a large canvas type anchor bag sporting a synch cord. Once the ladder sections were assembled, we loaded the bag with large rocks (as per instructions) so we could weigh down the bigger than life, donut resembling structure, and waded out to place it in its proposed resting place. Now floating in six feet of water, it was time for the fun to begin.

The two boys, Mario and Niklas, ten and eight years old respectively, quickly grabbed onto the ladders and hoisted themselves onto the top of the floating rubber bouncer and waited for me to climb aboard. They were smiling ear to ear from atop their new oversized lake toy. It was my turn to join them.

They made it look easy, climbing up the loose ladders, barely moving the gargantuan rubber raft from where it rested. I grabbed the top rung of the ladder while using my feet to find the bottom rung. Apparently, the tube was not the only thing out there that was gargantuan. My stomach was in the way of an easy climb. Once I got my foot on the bottom rung, I started to hoist up my 200 plus pound frame when I immediately saw the other side of the Bouncer come out of the water, rise at a 45-degree angle, sending me deeper into the water on the opposite side. There was only one way up on the tube, and I was not going to be embarrassed by NOT getting up on it. No Way! By now, the grandsons were giggling a little too much.

I tried again to get a solid foothold, grabbing the top rung and pulling myself up on the floating tube. Again, the opposite side came roaring out of the water like an orca whale in heat, splashing water down on me, and sending the two boys sliding off into the warm waters of Bauneg Beg Lake. Now the giggling turned to laughing out loud. I even used the boys as counterweights in my futile efforts to get on the tube. After the fifth try, I knew there was no way I was getting on that bouncer. Of course, the kids thought this was hilarious. Well, I showed them.

Wading back to the beach area, I got on my 2006, Bombardier,

Sea-Doo, GTX Supercharger jet ski, pulled up alongside the floating rubber raft, tied it off to a ladder rung and jumped on. I had made it. Okay, I wasn't proud of the way I did it.

Once onboard, I had rolled involuntarily to the center of the tube, bringing both boys crashing down in the center with me. Geez, how heavy was I? After the laughing and drooling stopped, I got off the floating raft that would never again see me on its mesh surface. I still own the bouncer and the kids still climb on and have fun each summer. They still invite me out there with them, but only because they know I can't get myself on it. Me? Well, I usually sit on my canopy-covered deck overlooking the unconquerable bouncer and have a drink. I love summers here on Bauneg Beg Lake. I hate the bouncer?

TWO: LIFE JACKET LILLY

On those long summer days, it's not unusual for me to go visit The Mayor and enjoy a cold beverage while we sit on his front lawn overlooking the beautiful warm waters of Bauneg Beg Lake. One day, while standing on my 36-foot long, 4-foot wide, Floe aluminum dock, I heard The Mayor call over, "Hey buddy, are you thirsty?" Before I knew it, I was going over to find him to enjoy a cold brew.

I jumped on my Bombardier jet ski and motored over to his dock to tie up. Unbeknownst to me, he had two of his granddaughters there visiting for the day. That was my first *experience* with six-year-old Lilly. No sooner did I tie up the jet ski to his dock when I heard Lilly say, "Where is your life jacket?" She continued, with hands on her hips, "It's not safe if you're not wearing your life jacket!" The Mayor was laughing about all this, as I didn't know what to say. Here I was, being scolded by a six-year-old I'd never met, and I didn't even have a beer in my hand yet.

The only thing I could do was promise Lilly I wouldn't ever go without my life jacket again. At least, when I knew she was on the lake. I noticed that whenever Lilly was in the water, she had a life jacket on. After being taken down a peg, I did enjoy a beer with her grandfather. (I think he's afraid of her too.) On leaving, I immediately put on my life jacket and showed Lilly I had learned the error of my ways. You know, sometimes kids can teach you something. Every time I see Lilly, I think of that day and the lesson she taught me. I pity Lilly's boyfriend when she starts dating. Maybe he can have a beer with The Mayor.

THREE: THE FRIENDLY SNAKE

It was late morning, and I was sitting at my desk at the Portsmouth Naval Shipyard, as the Public Works Department Planning Supervisor for the world's most powerful Nuclear Navy. (Now you know my background). It was a warm day, and I thought I'd go home early as I knew it would be a beautiful day on Bauneg Beg Lake. I left at noon, knowing my grandsons would be there along with other visiting family members.

When I got home, I was surprised to see all the kids standing on the sandy beach looking excitedly in and around the dock. My eldest grandson, Mario, was standing on the deck of the house overlooking the excitement below. I asked him, "What's everybody doing?" He replied, "There's a big snake in the water and I'm not going back in there."

I didn't blame him and went down the steps to the lawn to ask my wife and sister-in-law what all the commotion was about. They explained that a three foot black snake with a wide white band in the center of its long body was swimming around the dock. The peculiar thing was that the snake was not afraid of humans and seemingly wanted to play with the kids. Really? A playful snake? Here on Bauneg Beg Lake?

After a few minutes, I saw the snake swim from under the wooden dock and come straight toward my sister-in-law. It swam right up to her, slowly, as if it wanted to be picked up. Yeah, like that was going to happen. It was time for me to get into the action, so I went into the cottage to don my snake-capturing bathing suit and try to corner The Serpent of Bauneg Beg Lake. Didn't know we had one, did you?

On returning to the waterfront, ready for action, I noticed Mario had come down to the lawn too. I retrieved my wood-handled fish net from the cellar and came looking for the Beast of the East. I looked everywhere around the docks and in the weeds near the beach front. My wife and her sister had also lost visual sighting of the creature. We couldn't resume play knowing the snake was still on the loose.

No sooner did I come out of the water when I saw the snake. It was sunning itself on the lawn not five feet from where Mario was standing, unbeknownst to the grandson, of course, otherwise we were looking at a serious diaper change. Slowly, I approached Mario and led him away from the area as if nothing was going on. Then the Creature from the Deep slithered away into the warm lake water. He was in fact about three feet long, black with a white stripe (about 8 inches long) in its center, and seemed unafraid of people. When I put my net near the water, he actually swam toward me and into the net. The holes were too large to hold him and he easily swam through the holes and away from me. I followed him into the weeded area of the lot next door and on my last sighting, I saw him swimming away towards deeper water. I guess he figured he had played us out.

Unfortunately, several days later, I found a large section of the snake floating on my beach. It appeared that some local fisherman had caught him and cut him up for bait. I say that because the piece was knife cut.

After talking it over with the family, we think the snake might have been a pet that was no longer wanted and set free to fend for itself, or had escaped its pen. But on that eventful day, the kids cautiously reentered the warm waters of Bauneg Beg Lake and continued enjoying the warm, sunny day, talking about the friendly snake that had come their way. I did tell them about finding part of the snake days later. I wanted them to have a good memory of the encounter, but have no further fear of entering the warm water of the lake.

FOUR: HEAVY WEIGHT

Several years ago, we had purchased our first three-person towable. It was a large blow up vinyl, mesh-covered tube, sporting multi seats with handles that was almost as big as a small boat. The grandkids were growing up, and it was time to up the ante in the *fun* department. The kids would climb on and sit or kneel in any of the three seat areas with its formed slanted backrest, and I would pull them over the warm waters of (you guessed it) beautiful Bauneg Beg Lake. We all had a great time enjoying the monster tube. Even their parents climbed on for a ride around the lake. It was more enjoyment than they could get at any local amusement park. Well, for free anyway.

One day, late in the summer, the two grandsons, Mario and Niklas, asked me if I wanted to go on the tube with them. Being an expert boat handler, it had always been my job to drive the boat, not to be towed by one. Now, the trick was asking my wife, their grandmother, if she would drive the boat for our excursion around the lake. It didn't take too much coaxing for her to agree. When it came to her boys, she was a pushover. Even she had been on the tube for a ride around the lake at one time. Now it was my turn.

I donned my size 48-56 inch, adult sized, blue and black, Coast Guard Approved life jacket and rigged the tube to the rear of the pontoon boat. Once the two boys were seated on each side of the towable, I maneuvered my 200 plus pound frame in the center seat. I was ready. Well, not so fast, as luck would have it. When I finally seated myself in the center seat, the towable hit pay dirt, and we were sitting on beach sand in shallow water. I got out, floated the tube to deeper water and got on again. How embarrassing! Of course, the two boys couldn't help making some remark about the *false start*. The little NASCAR freaks!

We were finally floating and ready to go. We gave the boat driver the thumbs up, and we were off. I could hear the 75 hp Mariner engine rev up, trying to pull us to the top of the water. The atmosphere was filled with excitement. We were seconds from flying around the lake at NASCAR speeds! We didn't get 50 feet when the tube started shaking and jerking around and having a hard time getting up on the surface of the water. Then, everything broke loose. No... *everything* broke loose!

While still under strain, the front harness, made of military grade, reinforced, quarter-inch thick, four-inch wide, nuclear indestructible nylon webbing that could hold Godzilla, tore away from the tube, leaving us floating like a bobber on a fishing pole, as we watched the boat pull away. I was living *Gilligan's Island* on my now injured towable. Geez, how heavy was I? The two boys (the Skipper and the Professor) couldn't stop howling. I laughed too. It was funny. Luckily, the harness had a back-end loop, so we were easily returned to the dock. My ride (and only ride) was 50 feet. Maybe that diet isn't looking so bad after all.

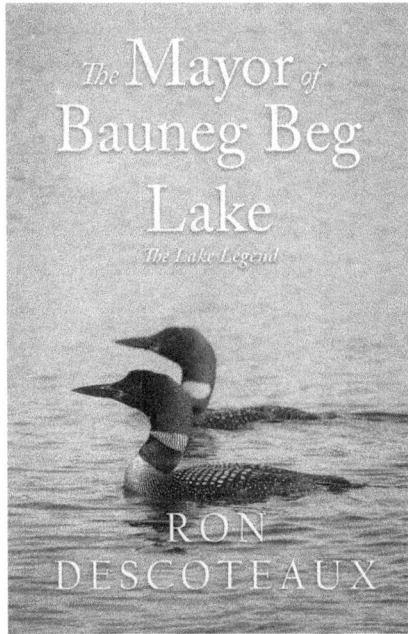

A FREE short story from
The Mayor of Bauneg Beg Lake
The Lake Legend...

PAKISTAN VISITS BAUNEG BEG LAKE

Southern Maine had just endured its third heavy snowstorm over a ten-day period. The snow was over three feet high on the normally green lawns, and our beautiful lane was narrowed down to one car width in some places. Most cottage roofs were heavily laden with a thick blanket of snow crying for attention. Winter was dealing a hard blow to New England, and especially on our little lake in South Sanford. What was one to do? Regardless of the weather conditions, the lake faithful were aware that there were only 58 days to dock in on the shores of Bauneg Beg Lake. Even Mother Nature could not stop the lake from watering out in its appointed season. In the meantime, despite the weather, there were things to be done, shopping to do, people to see, places to go. Today... it was online shopping day.

It was last year that I had purchased a large flag from The American Flag Company for a mere $35. It was a 4 x 6 foot triple-stitched heavy-duty nylon flag made to withstand a nuclear assault and other natural disasters it may encounter. One day, The Mayor, obviously envious of my larger (than his) flag, asked about it. I told him where I got it and answered his question about the cost. That same day, The Mayor let me know that he had just purchased the same exact flag for half price on Amazon. Really, mayor? Why do you have to be like that? After two weeks, most people in the cove, with The Mayor's help, had the same flag for half the cost that I paid for mine. I thought maybe mine would last twice as long since I paid double for it. Yeah... probably not. It was then, however, The Mayor told me, "Whenever you want to buy something, check it out on Amazon, and I will get it for you, free shipping. Anytime buddy." Well, the day was here... buddy!

For Christmas, I had received two $50 Amazon gift cards from my mom. My brother was an Amazon buying addict, not me, but knew that one day I may have use for them. I knew Mom needed some safety items for her home to help her in her advancing years. She had mentioned some items, and I thought that buying them on Amazon was a good idea. Her thoughtful gift would now come back to her for her enjoyment. Knowing what I wanted, I contacted The Mayor, who agreed to help me get my items on his free shipping account. So one cold, bright sunny morning, I was off to visit the lake mayor and get my shopping done. My inner child was giddy with anticipation. (We are getting along better lately.)

Armed with my two gift cards, I sat next to The Mayor who sat at his command post in front of his larger-than-life geriatric computer screen, and large bright green-colored, backlit keyboard that would have served as a night light anywhere, or for a warning beacon for ships at sea. The Mayor was battle-ready for Amazon.

I helped him navigate to the two items that I wanted, which he skillfully added to his *cart*. Then it was time to pay for my much anticipated items. I got the first gift card out and started to peel back the small strip to expose the fourteen thousand digit code that would activate the card (or some nuclear missiles in Nevada) and reduce the price of my purchase. Using my Navy folding jack knife, I began scratching off the sticky strip that held the secret number. I scratched and scratched… and scratched, only to find I was going through the plastic card with no number showing. The Mayor thought it might be imbedded deeper and applied Goo-Gone to see if we could expose the magic money making number. Of course, that didn't go well either. The number was just not there to be found. So, the next step was to call Amazon Customer Service. I don't know how much business The Mayor does with Amazon, but they knew his first name. That's a good thing, right?

The Mayor called the all too familiar customer service number (from his speed dial no less) and waited for the automated menu to direct his call to the right Amazon support person located in some unknown country. (Even Amazon has no idea where their service representatives live.) Within several seconds, a nice lady introduced herself as Maria and offered to help. That conversation went something like this: (Speakerphone was on.)

Maria: "My name is Maria, and I will be helping you today."

Mayor: "Okay."

Maria: "This call may be recorded because I'll forget why you called. What is your name, account number, your address, last year's income, and the weight of your second-born child so we can verify you are who you say you are?"

Mayor: "Okay, but it's already on file."

Maria: "Okay, thank you Roger. Can I call you Roger? What can I do to make your day better?"

Mayor: "I have a gift card that has no code number on the back. We removed the sticky strip, but did not find the number I need to activate the card on a purchase I'm trying to make."

Maria: "Okay, Roger, I apologize for this inconvenience. However, I think you're lying, so I will need you to send me a picture of the card, so Cassim, in our security department, can look it over and make a determination if we will honor your request."

Roger: "Okay, you want me to send you a picture of the card, is that right?"

Maria: "Yes. I will send you my email address. You can send the picture of the card, and we will get back to you. Okay, Roger?"

Roger: "Okay, but how long will that take?"

Maria: "We will have Cassim do the work right away and will get back to you very quickly. Okay, Roger?"

Roger: "Okay." He hung up the phone. He then took a photo of the defective card with his cell phone, transferred the picture to his laptop, then to an email Maria sent him with the appropriate email address to some unknown Amazon Service area. I was hoping Cassim was not milking his cow or out planting corn on his parent's meager plot in the Pakistan countryside.

After several minutes, The Mayor got tired of waiting for the "fast response" and decided to give the Amazon Customer Service call another try. This time was somewhat different, though:

Service Rep: "This is Amazon service area. How can I help you today?"

Roger: "Yes, I called earlier about my deficient gift card. Can I speak to Maria please? Is Maria there? She had me send her a picture of the card so Cassim could look it over and accept the card."

Service Rep: "Roger, is that you? This is Cassim!" (Not really Cassim, but it could have been, just go with it.)

Roger: "Is Maria there? She gave me an email address, and I sent her a picture of my bad gift card so someone at Amazon could credit my account."

Cassim: "Hello Roger, I am very sorry for your troubles. I can help. Please send me a photo of the bad card and I will have our department work on it right away. Okay, Roger?"

Roger: "I already sent a picture of the card to Maria, but okay, I'll send you another one."

Cassim: "Okay, thank you Roger."

Roger: "How long will this take?"

Cassim: "Once I get the photo, I can see what changes I can help you with, okay Roger? I am very sorry for your inconvenience, Roger. Please stay on the line, Roger."

A few minutes passed while Cassim looked over the bad card. He promised Roger that he would have it settled within a few days and Roger would find the credit on his account. In the meantime, the end of the conversation went like this:

Cassim: "Because of your inconvenience today, I will be giving you a $10 credit on your account Roger." (Which appeared instantly on The Mayor's account.)

Roger: "Okay, thank you."

Cassim: "Roger, how did I do to help you today? Are you satisfied?"

Roger: "You did a good job."

Cassim: "Wooohoooo, thank you so much Roger. I did a good job for you today! Yeehaaa!"

In the background, I heard Cassim say, "Nishka, put the cow back outside please, and get your brother in here to clean up this mess."

It was within an hour that the bad gift card had been made good, and the money was placed in Roger's Amazon account. Thank you, Amazon. Thank you, Roger... and thank you, Cassim!

Life was good again on Bauneg Beg Lake.

NOTE: I had a second card that had no online problems, and the order went through with free shipping. So, it all ended well. Working the issue through Amazon was an experience for sure. In the end, they came through. I was happy. The Mayor was happy. And Mom was the happiest. If not, I'll send her stuff to Cassim and his cow.

about the author

This is Ron Descoteaux's fifth book about the life and times on the lake he calls his home. The first four books were a series entitled *Living the Life on Bauneg Beg Lake*. His humorous true adventures are told with his own manner of sometimes sarcastic wit all taking place in southern Maine, but could actually be on any lake, in any state.

Ron lives on Bauneg Beg Lake in southern Maine with his wife Jeannine. They are the proud parents of two grown children, a son and a daughter. They also have five adult grandchildren and two beautiful great grandchildren.

Retiring in 2010 after more than forty years of government service, little did they know what adventures would come their way, living near the busy Corbin Way boat ramp. Over the years, Ron has written countless true stories about himself, friends, family, and visitors who have come across his path in those wonderful events and circumstances that sometimes make you scratch your... well, you know.

Ron is currently the deputy buoy tender on the lake. He provides summer long weekly inspections of the 18 buoy system and keeps logs on any and all buoy activities. He provides all that data to the State Navigation Office each year for the Board of Trustees.

He and his wife have enjoyed thirty years on the lake giving thanks to God every day for their little piece of heaven on earth.

behind the author

I am very fortunate that my friend and neighbor is also my "coach" for the books I write. The term "coach" was a term of endearment I bestowed on her after she agreed to take on most of the work that is needed to get a book published. It takes countless hours of reading, editing, upgrading, formatting, uploading, working with the cover company, and working toward the final assembly of the books I was looking for. To date, Coach has published four books for me in the *Living the Life on Bauneg Beg Lake* series. This is significant for a woman who is herself a professional author and has her own series of books on the shelf. Fortunate? I would say so.

Jennifer Rogers was instrumental in keeping me on track and overseeing all aspects of each project, to the smallest details, until the books came to fruition. Jennifer is an exemplary and masterful author and willingly shares her God-given talents with anyone seeking her guidance. She has an infectious positive attitude, outstanding work habits, is very expedient in her work and does it right the first time. Her hard work on my behalf has made this journey a pleasant and joyful one, even as she pens her own highly entertaining adventures into other realms. This will be my fifth book in the skillful care of her sharp wit.

Jennifer has authored her own published books. Her first trilogy was the well written *Ariboslia* series, including the titles *Astray*, *Adrift*, and *Aloft*. Those entertaining Christian fantasy works were followed up with *Alight*. While her heroin travels to far off realms, God plays a big role throughout the adventure. She artfully seeks out God in her travels... and HE responds. Jennifer has also written a heartwarming page turner, *The Smeraldo Flower*. She has most recently released her second adventurous *Cursed Lands* Trilogy. Those novels consist of the highly entertaining *The Kings Curse* followed by *The Witch's Curse* and culminating with *The Queens Curse*. Again, her heroin is dependent on God for guidance and good judgement as she travels through unknown realms. Her books are written for all ages to enjoy and are highly entertaining. All of her works are available on Amazon and I highly recommended them for all members of the family. Her latest work, *Date with Death*, is still in the works and promises to be another great page turning adventure.

Jennifer and her husband Rick and their puppy, Tuki, live here as part of the Bauneg Beg Lake family. Her signature motto is: "You are loved", and she lives it every day.

acknowledgments

Having previously authored four books of life events from my southern Maine lake house, I find myself in a very content place in my geriatric years. This is my fifth and final book. I am truly living the life that I write about. Every day is a gift, and being able to live and witness every moment of this fantastic journey is also a gift I don't take lightly. Along the way, I have made friends and met so many wonderful people that have become part of my lake family. I could never share or publish these memoirs without the help of the characters within and support of a lot of wonderful people who bring them all to life for you and me to enjoy. So, with heartfelt gratitude....

- I first want to thank my lovely wife, Jeannine, for her unwavering support. She has read and edited every story, oftentimes more than once, keeping me from any lawsuits. Thank you, Honey!
- I want to thank my friend, neighbor, author, and "Coach", Jennifer Rogers, who graciously started me on the journey to publish my work. Her enthusiastic encouragement, guidance, and hands-on effort were invaluable in achieving what I never thought possible, all the while mastering her own creative writing. Thank you, Jennifer, for all your hard work.
- The drive to write about life on the lake came from friendships we share here. I want to thank each of the "characters" who allowed me to use their lake persona and some creative poetic license in the telling of these stories.

Thank you, Special K, the sheriff, The Mayor and Mrs. Mayor, Limoncello Bob, Patti Girl, Lady Gaga, The Botanists, The Plumber, The Architect, The Nurse, Mr. Sound Effects, The Black Russian, Tarzan, Salty, Two Lakes Over and The Lake Princess. You made all these stories come alive.

- I want to thank my friend and lake neighbor, Steve Bekeritis, for the many photos in this book. Most of the photos were carefully taken on Bauneg Beg Lake. He skillfully captures some of Mother Nature's most delicate creations. Thank you, Steve.

- And a special thank you to the crew from 100 Covers for being patient, professional, timely and instrumental in attaining the cover that exemplifies lake life in southern Maine. Thank you!

- And finally, thanks to God who set the road before me, and made the path straight.

www.ingramcontent.com/pod-product-compliance
Lightning Source LLC
Chambersburg PA
CBHW061821040426
42447CB00012B/2751